CW00969651

Recipes for a
PERFECT SUNDAY LUNCH

RECIPES FOR A PERFECT SUNDAY LUNCH

Marie-Pierre Moine

Photography by
Linda Burgess

CONRAN OCTOPUS

To Pierre Moine, my father,
in whose kitchen at Le Boisseau I spend
many happy hours.

THANKS AND ACKNOWLEDGMENTS

For their help in making *Recipes for A Perfect Sunday Lunch* such an enjoyable book to write, I am deeply grateful to the following: Colin MacIvor, chief guinea pig and perceptive critic; Lewis Esson, whose approach to editing is as generous as it is thorough; Linda Burgess, Jane Suthering and Paul Welti whose respective combined talents resulted in such great photographs and design. I would also like to thank my agent, Barbara Levy, and all the team at Conran Octopus for being so nice to work with and so professional: Anne Furniss, Mary Evans, Louise Simpson and Jo Mead.

For inspiration, recipe ideas, hints and tricks of the trade I am indebted to the following, writers as well as keen cooks (in alphabetical order): Georgina Brady, Robert Carrier, Anna Del Conte, Henrietta Green, Alison Habershon, Michèle Kurland, Jean Moine, Pierre Moine, Anne-Sophie Naudin, Sri Owen, Rosa Pereira, Tim Pearce. I must also thank Clarissa Dickson-Wright for allowing me to browse freely in Books for Cooks, Liz Leigh for introducing me to Arto der Haroutunian's *Middle Eastern Cookery* and Elspeth Thom in whose house I first tasted Jane Grigson's Queen of Puddings two decades ago.

First published in 1993 by
Conran Octopus Limited
37 Shelton Street
London WC2H 9HN

Text copyright © 1993 Marie-Pierre Moine
Photography copyright © 1993 Linda Burgess
Design copyright © 1993 Conran Octopus
Limited

The right of Marie-Pierre Moine to be identified as the author of this work has been asserted by her in accordance with the Copyright, Designs and Patents Act 1988.

All rights reserved. No part of this work may be reproduced, stored in a retrieval system or transmitted in any form or by any means, electronic, electrostatic, magnetic tape, mechanical, photocopying, recording or otherwise, without the prior permission in writing of the publisher.

Both metric and imperial quantities are given in the recipes. Use either all metric or all imperial, as the two are not interchangeable.

Art Director Mary Evans
Designer Paul Welti
Project Editor Louise Simpson
Editor Lewis Esson
Editorial Assistant Jo Mead
Production Controller Alison McIver
Home Economist Jane Suthering

A CIP catalogue record for this book is available from the British Library

ISBN 1 85029 450 X

Typeset by Servis Filmsetting Limited
Printed and bound in Hong Kong by Wing King Tong Co. Limited

CONTENTS

INTRODUCTION

I love Sunday lunch. Whatever the
season and the circumstances, it is the
one meal of the week when people really
have a chance to relax and enjoy good
food and conversation. For a while, time
stands still around the table as guests get
acquainted – or re-acquainted, as most
of us are far too busy to see a lot of each
other during the week.

Whether the Sunday lunch is a casual
sprawling family occasion or a more
formal grown-up affair, I always enjoy
the cooking involved. Sunday lunch is a
generous meal. Less fraught and
competitive than a dinner party, it is an
opportunity to indulge your guests – and
yourself. A pudding is called for and,
even before that, the fat and animal
protein content of the meal are allowed
to creep up just for once.

Sunday lunch is not really the place
for culinary experiments and interesting
surprises: it is a meal that should please
everybody – including lone vegetarians
who find themselves surrounded by
meat-eaters. Whenever possible, the
menus in this book accommodate that
growing vocal minority with alternative
suggestions that will allow them to join
in and not involve you the Cook, in too
much extra work. I have always felt
sorry for teenage vegetarians who had to
make do with bags of peanuts and
mounds of spuds while their carnivorous
relatives tucked into tender juicy lamb
or succulent chicken.

Last but not least, Sunday lunch does
not have to take place around 1pm on
Sunday. Friends of mine have theirs at
6pm in order not to break up their one
day of sport. If you prefer, you can even
do what some other friends do and have
your Sunday lunch early on Saturday
afternoon!

SHOPPING

Most of the *Recipes For A Perfect Sunday Lunch* can be cooked with good ingredients from a large quality supermarket . . . but (and this is a pretty big 'but') Sunday lunch *is* supposed to be an enjoyable occasion, and I have much more fun shopping in the less clinical and more relaxed surroundings of an open-air market or specialist shops, when time allows.

STAPLES AND FAVOURITE INGREDIENTS

This is not the place for a sermon on the well-stocked larder: I am assuming that you have at hand the right staples for your everyday needs, that you shop little and often for fresh seasonal produce and that you discard fading spices and jaded store cupboard ingredients every few months. What I would like to concentrate on instead are my own quirks and personal favourites.

Substitutes: wherever it seemed appropriate, I have suggested alternative ingredients. You will find that there is room for a little extra leeway if you cannot get hold of something or hate the flavour of, say, dill.

Chicken: corn-fed or free-range birds are worth every single extra penny they cost.

Stock: some supermarkets now sell chilled fresh stocks – these are not cheap but are worth buying and freezing when you feel 'in pocket'. Also ask your butcher for 'boiling birds', – tougher and older hens that are wonderful for making stock. Remove some of the meat after the bird has been simmering for about 50 minutes to make a meal of the bird as well as stock. Fish stock may be made in 15 minutes (any longer will

spoil the flavour) with crustacean shells, the bones and trimmings from non-oily white fish, a few sprigs of herbs and a little lemon zest. Onions or shallots chopped and simmered with a few sprigs of herbs and one or two stalks of celery or a little fennel make a very easy vegetable stock – far lighter than the generally over-salted stock cubes.

Oils: groundnut or sunflower seed are the best all-purpose neutral-flavoured cooking oils. Also have a small bottle of sesame seed oil for stir-frying, and two kinds of olive oil, ordinary for everyday uses and a strong extra virgin oil for those recipes when a good olive taste is of the essence.

Butter: I love the taste of good salted country butter on fresh bread, but sweet unsalted butter is more versatile in cooking. You can compromise with a lightly salted variety.

Cream & Co.: we seem to have become a cream-free household. In my everyday cooking I substitute Greek-style yogurt and/or fromage frais. Lower fat cream cheese is worth experimenting with. High in fat – but hard to beat for flavoursome creaminess – is Mascarpone, available in Italian delis and good supermarkets (check the use-by date on the tub, since turnover can be rather slow).

Cans: artichoke hearts, water chestnuts, haricot beans (flageolets and white beans) and petits pois are always useful for starters and side dishes.

Herbs: a kitchen without fresh herbs is like a living room without fresh flowers – unlived in. Any 'disposable' food budget cash I am left with seems to be spent on fresh herbs, particularly flat-leaf parsley, chives, thyme and basil. When times are hard I use a lot of spring onions instead. Some dried herbs are better than others (oregano, marjoram, sage, bay, rosemary, thyme,

tarragon) but none should be kept longer than a few months.

Flavourings: I use a lot of harissa, the hot pepper sauce of North Africa. It is fiery, but more rounded than most other chilli condiments. Harissa is available in small cans from many large super-markets, delis and Oriental stores. Once opened, transfer it to a glass jar or plastic container and keep it in the refrigerator along with anchovy paste or purée (rather than essence). Tabasco is a possible substitute for harissa as are Oriental or South American chilli pastes. Perhaps my favourite flavour is that of citrus. I always keep several unwaxed lemons and limes, some at room temperature for squeezing, some in the refrigerator for slicing and zesting – I am a total sucker for any new zesting gadget on the market. Citrus or lemon pepper is also worth storing and I am seldom without a few stalks of fresh lemon grass, which I buy when I see it in supermarkets or Oriental stores and keep chilled (see Moroccan Chicken on page 95).

EQUIPMENT

In London I operate in a (truly) tiny galley kitchen, so appliances and utensils are kept to a minimum: a gas cooker with an efficient grill and a tried and trusted *batterie de cuisine*. I try to keep the latter from cluttering up every available inch of space, but I could not manage without a good set of knives, a small copper saucepan for sauces, a much-used wok, several pairs of scissors, spatulas, slotted spoons, a tiny spoon whisk as well as a large balloon one, pasta tongs (a good all-purpose tool), a couple of sieves (with fresh muslin to line them), a colander and three chopping boards (one large, one small and one dedicated exclusively to uncooked meat).

I also have a Magimix 3000 food processor with a spare set of bowls and I give thanks for its presence on a daily basis. There is no room left for a microwave in my kitchen but I do have a basic appliance just outside, a bit unloved but nevertheless useful for re-heating (and sometimes for cooking fish fillets and comforting coddled eggs).

A FEW REMARKS ABOUT ROASTING

When it comes to the traditional Sunday roast, families (whatever their political sympathies) suddenly turn very conservative . . . Every cook has her or his favourite methods and habits, so I know I am treading on sensitive ground here. Since this book is neither a compendium of traditional Sunday roasts nor a cookery course, the following remarks are humbly offered as shorthand guidelines to help readers who may like to follow some of the recipes while sticking to the expected roast for the main meat course.

Allow at least 250g/8½oz uncooked weight meat and bone per person or 125g/4½oz boneless meat, and plenty of time to bring meat to room temperature before roasting. Always preheat the oven to the required temperature – this takes time. My home oven takes a good 10 minutes to get really going. Use a trivet or roasting rack over the pan to ensure even roasting and remember to baste the meat a few times during cooking. Most roasts, particularly the larger ones, will carve and taste better if they are allowed time to settle in the switched-off hot oven with the door open after cooking. Larger roasts (2.3k/5lb and upwards) tend to cook more evenly and to keep more pleasingly moist if cooked at lower temperatures (1 or 2 stops down) than small or medium pieces of meat.

Chicken: 20 minutes on 230C/450F/gas8, then breast side down for 20 minutes at 180C/350F/gas4. Turn over again and continue roasting at the same temperature for 35-60 minutes depending on size. Baste very frequently, especially during the last 30 minutes of cooking.

Duck: 30 minutes on 230C/450F/gas8, then breast-side down at 160C/325F/gas3 for 20 minutes. Turn round again and continue roasting for another 50-60 minutes, depending on size.

Beef: roast on 230C/450F/gas8 for 20 minutes, then turn down to 180C/350F/gas4 and roast for about 15 minutes per 450g/1lb for rare, 20 minutes for medium and 25 minutes for well done.

Lamb: part-boned leg of young lamb cooks well gigot-style on 230C/450F/gas8 for 15-20 minutes per 450g/1lb, depending on how pink you like your lamb. More mature lamb may be better cooked more slowly on 230C/450F/gas8 for 25 minutes, then on 160C/325F/gas3 for 20 minutes per 450g/1lb for slightly pink lamb.

Pork: score well through the skin all over and cook on 180C/350F/gas4 for 35 minutes per 450g/1lb, then score again, sprinkle with fat and turn up to 230C/425F/gas8 for 10-15 minutes to glaze and crisp the crackling.

Recipes for a Perfect Sunday Lunch is based on menus which cater for different seasons and occasions, but the recipes work equally well individually and in their own right. You may like to experiment with your own mixing and matching. Even if you find it hard to wean family and friends away from the traditional Sunday roast, perhaps you could train them very gently by introducing new appetizers, starters and side dishes . . . . The idea is that Sunday lunch, whatever form it takes, should be enjoyed by all.

Appetizers and Starters

Vive l'apéritif! Especially before a convivial lunch. I hate rushing and much prefer the party to get going before the meal. The following recipe ideas – including a few liquid suggestions – are some of my favourite ways of keeping people happy before they sit down at the table. The dishes also work well as starters or as part of a buffet.

The Hot Quails' Eggs on page 106-7 also make good appetizers.

PISSALADIÈRE

SERVES 8-12

3 tbsp good-quality fruity olive oil, plus
* more for dribbling and serving*
900g/2lb Spanish onions, thinly sliced
1 tsp sugar
2-3 garlic cloves, crushed
few sprigs of thyme, snipped
1 tsp marjoram
½ tsp oregano
12 canned anchovy fillets in oil, drained
* and finely chopped*
1 tbsp cream cheese
30g/1oz freshly grated Parmesan cheese
8-12 sweet ripe cherry tomatoes, halved
6 black olives, stoned and chopped
several basil leaves, coarsely snipped
salt and freshly ground black pepper

FOR THE PASTRY:
200g/7oz cream cheese
200g/7oz slightly salted butter
325g/11oz plain flour, plus extra for
* dusting*
pinch of salt
pinch of paprika

First make the pastry: in a food processor fitted with the metal blade, whizz together the cream cheese and butter until smooth and creamy. Add the flour, a pinch each of salt and paprika and whizz again until the dough comes together in a rough ball. Wrap in film and chill for at least 30 minutes.

Make the topping: in a large heavy-based sauté pan or frying pan, heat 2 tablespoons of olive oil. Add the onions and sweat them gently over a low heat, stirring frequently. After a few minutes, cover and cook gently for about 20 minutes until soft and pale gold, checking frequently to make sure that the onions do not burn.

Add the remaining tablespoon of oil to the pan, together with the sugar, garlic, herbs, anchovy and cream cheese.

Adjust the seasoning and continue cooking the onion mixture very gently for another 10 minutes, stirring occasionally.

About halfway through the cooking of the onions, preheat the oven to 190C/375F/gas5 and oil a large square or rectangular baking sheet.

On a lightly floured surface, roll out the pastry fairly thinly and spread it on the baking sheet.

Prick the pastry with a fork in several places and sprinkle with the Parmesan. Spoon the onion topping over the pastry, spreading it up to the edges with a palette knife. Arrange the cherry tomatoes over the onion. Season with a little pepper and bake for about 30 minutes, until the pastry is cooked through and the topping golden brown.

Pissaladière is good served warm or at room temperature. Just before serving, scatter the chopped olives and basil over the topping and dribble over a little olive oil. Cut into squares or rectangles, either bite-size or starter-size.

GARLIC MAYONNAISE

MAKES ½ PINT

yolk of 1 large egg
1 tbsp French mustard
1 large juicy garlic clove, crushed (or more
* to taste)*
1 tsp red or white wine vinegar
1 tbsp finely snipped chives (or more to
* taste)*
about 200ml/7fl oz groundnut oil or
* 150ml/¼pt groundnut oil and 3 tbsp*
* strongly flavoured olive oil*
few drops of lemon juice (optional)
sea salt and freshly ground black pepper

Put the egg yolk in a large bowl with the mustard, garlic, vinegar, chives and some seasoning. Cover with a very thin

film of oil and leave to stand at room temperature for at least 1 hour, without stirring.

Then wedge the bowl firmly in place on a mat of dampened paper towels and whisk the contents of the bowl until well mixed (I use a hand-held electric whisk). Still whisking, trickle in a few more drops of the oil. As soon as the oil has become opaque and blended into the mixture, trickle in a little more, still whisking all the time.

Continue adding the groundnut oil very slowly in this way, a few drops at a time, until the mixture thickens. Then start pouring in the oil in a continuous trickle, still whisking. If using olive oil, whisk it in once you have used up all the groundnut oil and the mayonnaise is already well emulsified. Carry on in this way until the mayonnaise is thick and glossy.

Adjust the seasoning and add a few drops of lemon juice, more garlic or snipped chives, if wished. Cover and chill until needed.

SALMON RILLETTES

SERVES 12

450g/1lb fresh salmon
2 bay leaves
several sprigs each of thyme and parsley
1 tsp sugar
1 tbsp white wine vinegar
225g/8oz smoked salmon off-cuts
225g/8oz unsalted butter, softened
juice of 1 large unwaxed lemon and the
* finely grated zest of ½ of it*
juice of ½ lime
freshly ground black pepper
cayenne pepper
paprika
Tabasco
rye bread, wheaten wafers or mild-
* flavoured tortilla chips, to serve*

Poach the salmon in just enough gently bubbling water to cover, together with the bay leaves, some of the herbs, the sugar and the vinegar. Cook for a few minutes only until just done (the flesh flakes readily when forked). Drain the salmon, pat dry with paper towels and leave until cool enough to handle.

Meanwhile, snip the smoked salmon into small strips, discarding all the unappetizing tough skin bits.

Carefully remove the skin and bones from the cooked salmon, then flake the flesh, discarding the skin and picking out any stray bones. Snip the rest of the parsley and pluck off the tiny thyme leaves.

Whizz together the smoked salmon, softened butter, snipped herbs, lemon and lime juice and grated lemon zest in a food processor. Do not over-process – the mixture should remain very coarse.

Whizz in the flaked salmon briefly, then taste and season generously with black pepper, cayenne, paprika and a dash of Tabasco.

Spoon the rillettes into a serving dish or bowl. Cover and chill for at least 2 hours, or up to 2 days, until needed.

Remove the rillettes from the refrigerator 1 hour before serving. Serve with rye bread, wheaten wafers or tortilla chips.

14

ROUILLE

SERVES 6

2-3 small red chilli peppers
2 garlic cloves, chopped
1 small thin slice of bread, crust removed
*   and broken into pieces*
1 egg yolk
1 tsp tomato paste
115ml/4fl oz good-quality olive oil
sea salt
paprika or cayenne pepper, if liked
hard-boiled quails' eggs, crudités, tiny
*   boiled new potatoes or croutons, to serve*

If the chillis are dried, soak them in cold water for a couple of hours.

Discard the stems and seeds of the chillis and chop the flesh.

In a food processor, whizz together the chopped chillis, garlic, bread, egg yolk, tomato paste and a little salt. With the machine still running, trickle in the olive oil until the sauce is thick and smooth. Adjust the seasoning, adding a little paprika or cayenne pepper to taste. Stir in a tablespoon of cold water.

Chill until ready to serve with the accompaniment of your choice.

ANCHOVY AND EGG DIP

SERVES 8

12 canned anchovy fillets in oil, drained
*   and chopped*
2 tbsp good olive oil
1 large hard-boiled egg, chopped
several sprigs of flat-leaf parsley, snipped
6-10 capers, drained
1 tsp English mustard
100ml/3 ½fl oz fromage frais
1 tsp lemon juice
few drops of Tabasco
sea salt and freshly ground black pepper
garlic croutons, grilled brioche rounds, or
*   pan-poached asparagus sprue spears (see*
*   page 55), to serve*

Whizz the anchovies in a food processor with the olive oil for a few seconds. With the machine still running, feed in the chopped egg, followed by the parsley and capers.

Once they are roughly mixed, add the other ingredients and whizz again. Adjust the seasoning, if necessary, and chill in the refrigerator until about 30 minutes before serving.

Serve with garlic croutons, grilled brioche rounds or spears of pan-poached asparagus sprue.

GUACAMOLE

SERVES 8

2 ripe avocados
juice of 1 lime
1 garlic clove, chopped
1 small spring onion or small bunch of
*   chives, snipped*
¼ tsp harissa
½ tsp ground coriander
¼ tsp ground cumin
1 tbsp Greek-style yogurt
1 tbsp olive oil
sea salt and freshly ground black pepper

Peel and coarsely chop the avocados. Whizz them in a food processor with the lime juice, garlic and spring onion or chives.

Add the rest of the ingredients and whizz again briefly until just smooth. Adjust the seasoning, if necessary – the flavours will go on developing.

Chill until needed. The lime juice will keep the guacamole looking fresh and green for several hours.

Right A fresh and appetizing trio: Anchovy and Egg Dip, Rouille, and Guacamole. Serve with a selection of accompaniments including firm young radishes, boiled baby new potatoes and crisp poached asparagus sprues.

Marinated feta cubes

SERVES 6-8

225g/8oz Feta cheese
100ml/3 ½fl oz good-quality strongly
flavoured olive oil
1 tsp dried marjoram
1 tsp dried thyme
½ tsp ground dried sage
1 garlic clove, crushed
½ tsp harissa
good pinch of paprika
freshly ground black pepper
lemon juice, to serve

Cut the cheese into 2cm/¾in cubes.

In a clean dry jam jar, combine the olive oil with the herbs, garlic, harissa and paprika. Taste and adjust the seasoning with pepper.

Add the cubes of Feta cheese one at a time. Shake to coat. Leave them to mature in the refrigerator for a few hours or overnight (the mixture will keep for several days).

Serve speared on wooden cocktail sticks, sprinkled with a little extra pepper or paprika and a few drops of lemon juice.

Use any leftover oil as a salad dressing.

Spiced nuts

SERVES 6-8

good pinch of mild curry powder or ground
cumin
115g/4oz mixed nuts, including almonds,
hazelnuts, walnuts, peanuts, etc
groundnut oil, for greasing
sea salt and freshly ground black pepper

In a clean dry jam jar, combine about 2 teaspoons of salt with a little black pepper and the curry powder or cumin. Add the nuts and shake the jar thoroughly.

Grease a medium-sized frying pan with a little oil and put over a moderate heat. Add the flavoured nuts and sauté them for a few minutes, stirring and shaking the pan continuously.

If not using them immediately, allow the nuts to cool and keep them in the tightly sealed jar.

Fromage blanc on rye

SERVES 6-8

225g/8oz fromage blanc or curd cheese
2 spring onions or shallots, finely chopped
1 garlic clove, crushed
small bunch of chives
sea salt and freshly ground black pepper
thin slices of rye bread, halved, to serve

Combine the cheese with the spring onions or shallots and the garlic. Season to taste.

Snip the chives into the mixture, stir and serve spread on thin half slices of rye bread.

FLAVOURED OLIVES

SERVES 6-8

115g/4oz mixed good-quality black and green olives
about 200ml/7fl oz red or white wine vinegar
1 1/2 tbsp olive oil
1/2 garlic clove, crushed
few sprigs of thyme, leaves plucked off and snipped
small pinch of dried oregano
citrus pepper
freshly ground black pepper

Put the olives in a jar or bowl. Cover with vinegar and leave to steep for an hour. Drain and pat dry.

Rinse and dry the bowl, then pour in the olive oil and combine it with the garlic, herbs and a smattering of citrus pepper. Season with a little black pepper. Add the olives to the mixture and toss until well coated.

Leave in a cool place for at least 1 hour before serving. The olives will keep for several days in the refrigerator.

Left Flavoured Olives, Tomato Crostini
and Prosciutto and Bresaola Rolls.

TOMATO CROSTINI

SERVES 8-10

1 ciabatta loaf or cold brioche
1-2 large juicy garlic cloves, chopped
white part of 1 large spring onion, chopped
225g/8oz canned chopped tomatoes, drained
3 tbsp olive oil, plus extra for dribbling
1/2 tsp dried oregano or marjoram
1/2 tsp dried thyme
2 basil leaves, snipped (optional)
1/4 tsp harissa (optional)
45g/1 1/2oz Parmesan cheese, grated
sea salt and freshly ground black pepper
more basil leaves, to garnish (optional)

Preheat the grill to hot and line the grill rack or pan with foil.

Slice the ciabatta (the slices should be no thinner than 1cm/1/2in and no thicker than 2cm/3/4in. If using brioche, make biscuit-size rounds with a small pastry cutter.

Whizz together the garlic, spring onions, tomatoes, oil, herbs, harissa and one-third of the Parmesan in a food processor. Taste and adjust the seasoning, if necessary.

Spread this mixture over the slices of bread or rounds of brioche, coating each generously right up to the edge to prevent it burning under the grill. Sprinkle with the rest of the Parmesan and dribble a little olive oil over the top of each.

Grill for 6-8 minutes, until the edges of the bread are golden and slightly crispy. Keep an eye on the crostini as they cook, and move them around so that they grill evenly. Leave to cool for a few minutes before serving garnished with basil leaves, if using.

If you prefer a more crusty finish, try baking them in an oven preheated to 200C/400F/gas6 for 8-10 minutes. Leave to settle in the oven for 15 minutes after baking.

PROSCIUTTO AND BRESAOLA ROLLS

SERVES 8-10

2 or 3 very thin slices of Prosciutto or Serrano ham
3 or 4 very thin slices of Bresaola
6 tbsp Mascarpone or cream cheese
1 tsp lemon juice
1/2 tsp dried oregano
paprika
freshly ground black pepper
olive oil, for sprinkling
black Flavoured Olives (see left), to serve
canned artichoke hearts, drained (optional)

Divide each slice of ham and Bresaola into 3 or 4 rectangles. Combine the cheese with the lemon juice and oregano. Season liberally with paprika and pepper.

Place a teaspoon of the flavoured cheese in the centre of each ham or Bresaola rectangle. Roll up tightly and chill until needed.

Sprinkle lightly with olive oil just before serving, spiked with a wooden cocktail stick. Serve with black Flavoured Olives.

Instead of making rolls, you can put a generous teaspoon of flavoured cheese in the centre of each of several drained canned artichoke hearts. Cover with a piece of ham or Bresaola, tucking in the edges neatly, or trimming them with scissors to neaten if easier.

MARGARITAS

MAKES 4

100ml/3 ½fl oz tequila
juice of 4 limes or lemons
100ml/3 ½fl oz orange-flavoured liqueur,
*   such as Cointreau, Curaçao or Triple*
*   Sec*
sea salt
twists or thin slices of unwaxed lime or
*   orange, to serve*

Chill the glasses. Rub the rims with a
cut lime or lemon, then dip them in sea
salt.

Half fill a cocktail shaker or jug with
crushed ice or ice cubes. Pour in the
tequila, lime or lemon juice and orange
liqueur. Shake well and pour into the
prepared glasses.

Add a twist or thin slice of lime or
orange, and extra ice, if liked.

RED FIZZ

SERVES 6

1 bottle of dry 'méthode traditionnelle'
*   sparkling wine*
about 450ml/¾pt freshly squeezed or
*   premium blood-orange juice*
6 cubes of cane sugar
2 tbsp brandy
few drops of Angostura bitters

Chill the wine and orange juice well.

Put a sugar cube in each of 6 flute
glasses. Pour over a teaspoon of brandy
in each.

Divide the sparkling wine between
the glasses. Top with orange juice and a
few scant drops of bitters.

FRUIT SPLASH

SERVES 6

225g/8oz mixed red berries, such as
*   raspberries or redcurrants, defrosted if*
*   frozen*
575ml/1pt sparkling apple juice
small bunch of mint
450ml/¾pt lemonade, chilled
caster sugar (optional)
1 unwaxed orange, thinly sliced
1 apple, thinly sliced and lightly brushed
*   with lemon juice*

Whizz the berries in a food processor
with a little apple juice and a few mint
leaves. Strain through a fine sieve into a
large glass jug. Pour in the remaining
apple juice and chill.

Just before serving, pour in the
lemonade and sweeten with sugar, if
wished.

Serve in tall glasses with plenty of ice
cubes, slices of orange and apple and
small sprigs of mint.

Right From alcohol-free to very boozy,
three colourful cocktails: Fruit Splash, Red
Fizz and Margarita.

INTIMATIONS OF SPRING

combining winter warmth with early spring produce

MENU

FOR 8

*Pot-luck Chicken
Sauce Verte
Sauce Rouge*

* * *

*Fruit Compote
Orange Cake*

22

THE days are getting longer . . . the air is clear but the wind still chilling . . . everyone shivers in fresh linens and cottons . . . this meal was devised in the early spring for those Sundays when the new season is fragile and the weather blustery. In super-markets, as usual weeks ahead of the world outside, shelves were bursting with early spring vegetables and fruit imported from warmer climes – all looking tempting, if somewhat premature.

This menu combines the old and the new in a flexible gutsy mix. I cook two small-to-medium chickens side by side in a squat fish kettle. This most serviceable of utensils was won years ago from a friend who resented the space it took as she only used it twice a year. I have smugly used it at least twice a month ever since. It sits comfortably on the hob across two rings and poaches evenly and quickly. The interior rack is great for lifting out intact awkward objects, such as chickens, from their cooking liquid. You will notice that I skin my birds first. To my mind chicken skin (unless of course it happens to be crisply roasted) has little to offer except a flaccid fatty chew.

Pot-luck Chicken is an easy dish to make and serve. There is only one caveat: take great care to simmer the birds very gently indeed. Uninsulated by skin, they will toughen all too easily if cooked rapidly. Choose the neatest freshest vegetables available and use plenty of them. The *mélange* is up to you, but for colour and bite try to include baby turnips, potatoes, large spring onions, small carrots with their fronds and a few spears of asparagus. The cooking times I indicate are for vegetables done a little more than *al dente*, so adjust them to your liking.

The Fruit Compote supports fresh fruit, not at its most exciting at this time of year, with dried fruit. The red fruit coulis tastes pleasingly sharp, and as an incidental bonus may also be a first step towards that murky seasonal task – Clearing The Freezer.

VEGETARIAN OPTION: for strictly vegetarian friends, I bring to the boil a separate pot of stock, using the same ingredients but without the chicken wings and bacon. Simmer for an hour, discard the flavourings and then poach the vegetables, allowing extra amounts.

SHOPPING: pancetta may be a little hard to find, but it is the same cut of meat as bacon, ie the belly of the pig, and you can use bacon instead. Get your favourite delicatessen to cut it wafer-thin.

TO DRINK: with this easy-going meal, give a choice of light red or white wine, and serve a fruity Gamay from Touraine or the Ardèche, together with an Australian Riesling. For the dessert, try a half-bottle of Orange Muscat, or serve each guest a finger of Cointreau on plenty of ice. Smoky Lapsang Souchong would make a good alternative to coffee, accompanied by an extra sliver or two of Orange Cake.

PLAN OF ACTION

The day before or earlier in the morning
Main course: make Sauce Rouge
Dessert: make Orange Cake and red fruit coulis for Fruit Compote

About 2 hours before the meal
Main course: make stock and Sauce Verte; skin chickens and prepare vegetables
Dessert: prepare fresh fruit
have all equipment and accompaniments ready

About 1 ¼ hours before
Main course: poach chickens

About ¾ hour before
Main course: prepare sausages

20-30 minutes before
Main course: cook vegetables

Just before eating
Main course: carve chicken; assemble

POT-LUCK CHICKEN

2 small-to-medium-sized free-range or
  corn-fed chickens
900g/2lb new potatoes
450g/1lb young carrots
450g/1lb baby turnips
2 small Savoy cabbages, quartered
450g/1lb broccoli florets
450g/1lb small leeks
450g/1lb thin green asparagus
225g/8oz baby sweetcorn (optional)
225g/8oz French beans or frozen broad
  beans
12 large spring onions
225g/8oz mange-tout peas
16 cocktail sausages
8-12 very thin slices of pancetta or good
  streaky bacon
few sprigs of flat-leaf parsley and chervil,
  snipped, to serve

FOR THE STOCK:
1 large Spanish onion, quartered
1 large carrot, peeled
2 celery stalks
1 bouquet garni (made with 2 sprigs each
  of flat-leaf parsley and thyme and 2 bay
  leaves)
6 black peppercorns
2 thick slices of rindless lean smoked back
  bacon
sea salt and freshly ground black pepper

TO SERVE:
small pickled gherkins
Meaux and English mustards

First prepare the stock: chop the wings
off the chickens. Bring to the boil about
1.8 litre/3¼ pt of water in a large pot.
Add the onion, carrot, celery, bouquet
garni and peppercorns. Bring back to
the boil then add the chicken wings and
bacon. Season lightly with salt and
simmer for 20 minutes.
    While the stock is simmering, skin
the birds and prepare the vegetables.

Add the skinned birds to the pot and
bring back to a gentle simmer. Poach,
keeping the bubbles low, for 1¼ hours
or until the birds are cooked through
and the juices run clear when the
thickest part of the flesh is pierced.
    After about 50 minutes of cooking,
grill the cocktail sausages until cooked
through but not burnt, keeping the heat
low to moderate. Drain on paper towels.
    Remove the cooked chickens from the
stock and keep warm. Strain the stock
into a large saucepan, return it to a
moderate boil and adjust the seasoning.
    Poach the vegetables in the stock:
starting with the potatoes; then about 5
minutes later add the carrots and
turnips; 7-8 minutes after that, drop in
the cabbage, broccoli and leeks, then 3-4
minutes later the asparagus, sweetcorn if
using, beans, the spring onions and
mange-tout peas. Cook the vegetables
until done almost to your liking (the
vegetables will go on cooking after you
have taken them off the heat). Drain
carefully before serving.
    While the vegetables are cooking,
wrap the cooked cocktail sausages with
pancetta or bacon and secure with a
wooden cocktail stick. Grill lightly until
golden. Then remove and discard the
sticks. Keep the sausages warm on paper
towels.
    To serve: heap the vegetables on a
large warmed dish. Joint the chicken
and arrange the pieces on the bed of
vegetables, together with the sausages.
Moisten all the contents of the dish with
a little hot stock and sprinkle liberally
with snipped fresh herbs.
    Serve accompanied by the remaining
hot stock in a warmed jug, pickled
gherkins, Meaux and English mustards,
coarse sea salt and black pepper and the
Sauce Verte and Sauce Rouge.

SAUCE VERTE

bunch of watercress, leaves only
several sprigs of flat-leaf parsley
1 tsp anchovy paste
450ml/¾pt strong Garlic Mayonnaise
  (see page 12)
citrus pepper

Reserving a few leaves, stew the
watercress and parsley with the anchovy
paste in 5 or 6 tablespoons of lightly
boiling water for 5-8 minutes. Push this
through a sieve and leave it to cool.
    Stir the juicy purée into the
mayonnaise, a little at a time, until
happy with the colour and taste. Snip in
the reserved leaves and season with a
little citrus pepper.

SAUCE ROUGE

2 large sweet red peppers, charred under a
  hot grill (see page 29), skinned and
  deseeded
4 ripe tomatoes, blanched, skinned and
  deseeded
3-4 tbsp extra virgin olive oil
few sprigs of coriander
1-2 tbsp fromage frais
sea salt and freshly ground black pepper

Chop the peppers and the tomatoes.
Combine with the olive oil and snip in
the coriander. Season and set aside for a
couple of hours.
    To serve, whizz in a food processor
or blender, add a little fromage frais
and whizz again briefly. Adjust the
seasoning, if necessary.

24

FRUIT COMPOTE

*350g/12oz frozen red fruit, such as
    raspberries, blackcurrants and
    redcurrants, defrosted*
*250g/8 1/2oz dried fruit, such as apricots,
    prunes, sultanas etc, rinsed*
*675g/1 1/2lb mixed seasonal and exotic
    fruit, such as grapes, apples, lychees,
    kumquats, mango or guavas, figs and
    early strawberries*
575ml/1pt weak Earl Grey tea
3 tbsp Cointreau, kirsch or rum
115g/4oz caster sugar (plus more to taste)
juice of 1 large lemon
*175ml/6fl oz each Greek-style yogurt and
    fromage frais, to serve*

Defrost the red fruit, rinse the dried
fruit and clean the mixed fresh fruit.

Bring the tea to a gentle simmer.
Poach the dried fruit in the tea until soft
and plump. Drain, reserving the
poaching liquid.

Sprinkle the drained fruit with a little
of the Cointreau, kirsch or rum.
Combine the sugar with the poaching
liquid and bring it back to a gentle boil.
Cook for a few minutes.

Whizz the defrosted red fruit in a
food processor. Take the light sugar
syrup off the heat. Push the red fruit
coulis through a sieve into the syrup and
stir in well. Reserve in a cool place.

Prepare the fresh fruit, cutting it into
attractive and manageable pieces.
Lightly combine these with the poached
fruit in a coupe or pretty dish. Sprinkle
the lemon juice over the fruit, together
with the remaining Cointreau, rum or
kirsch. Add a little more sugar, if liked,
and leave to steep in a cool place for 1
or 2 hours.

Serve the compote with the red fruit
coulis, the Greek-style yogurt and
fromage frais mixed in a bowl and slices
of Orange Cake.

ORANGE CAKE

115g/4oz caster sugar
*115g/4oz soft unsalted butter, plus extra
    for greasing*
2 large or 3 small eggs
115g/4oz self-raising flour
1 tbsp Cointreau
*2 tbsp orange juice and 2 tsp grated zest
    from an unwaxed orange*
icing sugar, for dusting

Preheat the oven to 190C/375F/gas5
and grease a 18-20cm/7-8in savarin pan
with butter.

Cream together the sugar and butter.
Whisk the eggs into the mixture. Sift in
the flour and fold it in. Stir in the
Cointreau, orange juice and zest.

Spoon the mixture into the prepared
mould, then knock the base of the pan
against a working surface to settle the
contents.

Bake for 20-30 minutes until the cake
is cooked and springy to the touch.
Stand upside down on a serving dish
and leave to cool in the pan for a few
minutes.

Carefully unmould the cake. Sprinkle
generously with icing sugar and leave to
cool completely.

Just before serving the cake cut in
thin slices and dust it again with a little
more icing sugar.

*Right To round off the meal after Pot-luck
Chicken and its condiments, put Orange
Cake and Fruit Compote on the table. The
moist and delicate Orange Cake can also be
served on its own, with coffee or at tea-
time. First glaze with a light orange syrup
(see Orange Tart Topping on page 85).*

SPICY SUNDAY ROAST

*a late-summer lunch with
Mediterranean overtones*

MENU

FOR 8

*Roast Leg of Lamb
with a Spicy Crust
Potato Galettes
Courgette and Tomato Gratin
Flageolets with Pepper Strips*

* * *

Caramel Apple Tart

How do you like your lamb? I seem to like mine less pink than most and always end up eating the end slices. As a family we have constant arguments over the cooking of lamb – some of us have even been known to tamper with the timer on the quiet to ensure that the lamb would be cooked just to our liking.

Whether you like your leg of lamb very pink or just a little rosy, I am of the opinion that it should roast in a very hot oven and rest in the switched-off oven for ten to fifteen minutes afterwards to allow the juices to flow back to the edges of the meat. Some people prefer to take it out of the oven and keep it warm (perhaps covered in foil) while it rests.

The last time I cooked this lunch for the family and a couple of old friends – out on the verandah of my father's house in the Loire – on a blazing hot day, I served ripe charentais melons as a light starter. Also, as I had found plenty of gloriously fresh purple garlic on the market, I added a little extra 'condiment' – garlic cream sauce – to serve alongside the gravy of lamb juices and white wine.

To make this sauce: in a small pan cover a couple of heads of fresh garlic with cold water. Bring to the boil, drain and rinse and then return to the boil in fresh cold water. Simmer for 15-20 minutes, or until tender. Drain well, allow to cool slightly and then squeeze the cloves until the creamy flesh pops out. Season this paste generously, add a dribbling of olive oil and a little fromage frais or double cream. Whisk and serve hot with the lamb. I promise that this creamy sauce will have the flavour of garlic, but none of the all-too-frequent pungent assertiveness.

As we lingered happily at the table looking at the roses in the garden, the Caramel Apple Tart was verandah-temperature by the time we finally got round to it.

Above *Roast Lamb with a Spicy Crust*.

VEGETARIAN OPTION: this is built into this menu: quantities allow for 2 vegetarians and 6 meat eaters.

SHOPPING: provided you have canned flageolets in the store cupboard and puff pastry in the freezer, you can give the supermarket a miss. Instead, enjoy a wander round your local market looking for vegetables and apples, and get your friendly butcher to trim the lamb to your liking.

TO DRINK: with the lamb serve a big sunny Châteauneuf-du-Pape, or an Australian Shiraz. Stay with this for the dessert, or produce a bottle of Calvados and some tiny liqueur glasses.

I sometimes whizz up an instant granita with plenty of crushed ice and a trickle of Calvados and serve it in chilled glasses.

PLAN OF ACTION

Earlier in the morning
Main course: coat lamb; cook and chill potatoes; char and marinate peppers (both can be prepared the day before if convenient); prepare Courgette and Tomato Gratin Dessert: defrost pastry if frozen; caramelize apples; bake tart

About 1 ½ hours before the meal
Main course: prepare Potato Galettes; have all equipment and accompaniments ready; cook lamb

20-30 minutes before
Main course: add gratin to bottom shelf of oven; combine flageolets with other ingredients

About 10-15 minutes before
Main course: turn off oven, but leave in lamb and gratin; cook galettes

Just before eating
Main course: grill galettes; heat flageolets; carve lamb; remove gratin from oven

ROAST LEG OF LAMB WITH A SPICY CRUST

1.35k/3lb leg of young lamb, part boned and trimmed
5 tbsp dry white wine, for basting
sea salt and fresh black pepper

FOR THE CRUST:
3 garlic cloves
1 tbsp Dijon or English mustard
1 tbsp sweet mustard
several sprigs of flat-leaf parsley
several sprigs of coriander
1 tsp coriander seeds
1 tsp ground ginger
1 tsp ground cumin
1 tsp harissa or hot chilli paste
1 tbsp breadcrumbs
1 tbsp olive oil
2 tbsp orange juice

Rub the lamb with pepper. Whizz together the ingredients for the crust in a food processor. Using a stiff pastry brush, spread the mixture over the meat and leave it to stand on a roasting pan rack at room temperature for a good 2 hours.

Preheat the oven to 230C/450F/gas8.

Season the lamb lightly with salt then roast for about 45 minutes to 1 hour, turning it over once during cooking and basting it with the wine and cooking juices.

Leave the lamb to settle for 10 minutes in the switched-off oven and a few minutes outside before carving.

FLAGEOLETS WITH PEPPER STRIPS

2 large red or yellow sweet peppers
about 2 tbsp olive oil
4 spring onions
675g/1 ½lb canned flageolets, drained
2 tbsp dry white wine
few sprigs of flat-leaf parsley
sea salt and freshly ground black pepper

Char the peppers under a hot grill or over a flame until blackened. Then remove their skins and seeds. Cut the pepper flesh into fine strips and sprinkle them with a little olive oil. Leave to stand for at least 1 hour.

Heat 1 tablespoon of olive oil in a saucepan. Snip in the spring onions, both white and green parts. Cook for 1 minute to soften, then add the flageolets together with the wine, the pepper strips and their oil. Heat through gently.

Season to taste and snip in a little parsley to serve.

COURGETTE AND TOMATO GRATIN

550g/1 ¼lb large firm courgettes
2-3 garlic cloves
about 3-4 tbsp olive oil
550g/1 ¼lb firm ripe tomatoes
few sprigs of fresh thyme
2 pinches of dried oregano
pinch of caster sugar
150g/5 ½oz goats' cheese, cut into thin
*   strips*
45g/1 ½oz freshly grated Parmesan cheese
few basil leaves
sea salt and freshly ground black pepper

Cut the courgettes lengthwise into slices about 6mm/¼in thick. Blanch for 2 minutes in lightly salted boiling water. Drain and pat dry with paper towels.

If cooking the gratin on its own, preheat the oven to 200C/400F/gas6. If serving it with the lamb, slide a shelf down to the bottom of the oven and follow the Plan of Action.

Halve one of the garlic cloves. Rub a large gratin dish with the cut garlic, then brush the dish generously with olive oil.

Spread a layer of courgette slices over the prepared dish. Slice the tomatoes fairly thinly and discard the seeds and some of the pulp. Spread a layer of tomatoes over the courgettes.

Crush the remaining garlic into a bowl. Pluck off the tiny thyme leaves, add the oregano and sugar and season lightly with salt and more generously with pepper.

Sprinkle a little of this seasoning mixture over the tomatoes. Then sprinkle them with a little olive oil. Repeat with another layer of courgettes, tomatoes, seasoning mixture and sprinkling of olive oil. Finish with a topping of slivers of goats' cheese, followed by a sprinkling of grated Parmesan and some pepper.

Bake for about 20-25 minutes, until the cheese is melting and very lightly coloured (the vegetables should still be a little firm). Snip over a few leaves of basil before serving.

POTATO GALETTES

4-5 large waxy potatoes in their skins,
*   weighing about 1.2k/2 ½lb in total*
1 large Spanish onion, grated or finely
*   chopped*
2 tbsp groundnut oil
45g/1 ½oz unsalted butter
sea salt and freshly ground black pepper

Bake or boil the potatoes in their skins until they are about three-quarters cooked. Drain, allow to cool and then peel and chill.

When well-chilled, coarsely grate the potatoes. Combine with the onion and season to taste.

Heat 1 tablespoon of the oil in each of 2 frying pans. Divide the butter between them and tilt the pans to combine the butter and the oil. Once the mixture is sizzling hot in each pan, divide the grated potato between the pans and pat it down to spread it evenly. Reduce the heat a little and cook for about 10 minutes.

Meanwhile, preheat the grill.

Place a heatproof dish over each pan and turn the potato galettes over into these dishes. Then brown them lightly under the grill for 3-4 minutes. Serve the galettes at once.

Right Caramel Apple Tart.

CARAMEL APPLE TART

125g/4 ½oz unsalted butter
150g/5 ½oz caster sugar
1k/2 ¼lb firm pink apples
225g/8oz puff pastry
1 small egg, lightly beaten
1 tbsp granulated sugar
fromage frais or Greek-style yogurt,
*   flavoured with a little Calvados, to*
*   serve (optional)*

Melt two-thirds of the butter in a *moule à manqué* pan on top of the stove over a moderate heat. Then remove from the heat and sprinkle in two-thirds of the sugar. Mix well and leave to cool.

Core all the apples and peel half of them. Cut all of them into 4 or 8 segments, depending on size, and arrange the segments neatly in tight concentric circles in the pan, alternating peeled and unpeeled chunks.

Sprinkle with the rest of the sugar and dot with remaining butter. Cook on top of the stove over a moderate heat for 20 minutes, until the juices reduce and the sugar turns into a light gold bubbling caramel.

Leave the apples to cool a little and preheat the oven to 220C/425F/gas7.

Roll out the puff pastry fairly thinly. Using the rolling pin, lift the pastry and place it over the apples, tucking it in between the apples and the pan. Brush the pastry lightly with a little beaten egg. Sprinkle with the granulated sugar and then prick with a fork.

Bake for about 20-25 minutes, until cooked through and golden.

Leave to cool in the pan until ready to serve. Place a serving dish slightly larger than the pan over the tart and carefully turn it over into the dish. Rearrange the apples, if necessary.

Serve warm, with fromage frais or yogurt, flavoured with a little Calvados.

SEAFOOD LOVERS' TREAT

*an elegant lunch for a
gourmet guest*

MENU

FOR 3 OR MORE

Sophisticated Hot Prawn Salad

* * *

*Sea Bass with Roast Fennel
Carrot and Potato Purée
Peas with Almonds and Lettuce
Strips*

* * *

*Chocolate Souffléed Puddings with
Ginger Sauce*

34

THIS menu is for a grown-up occasion, when you have a gourmet guest and want the lunch to be a little different. It is devised for three people, but can easily be scaled up for four – or even six.

The souffléed puddings may well come out a little gooey inside – hence their name. I sometimes serve them with whipped cream, which nobody ever turns down.

SHOPPING: my only suggestion is to check ahead with the fishmonger to ensure that sea bass is available.

TO DRINK: what could be nicer with the first two courses than a Gewürztraminer from Alsace? I prefer to savour the Chocolate Souffléed Puddings on their own or with sparkling water.

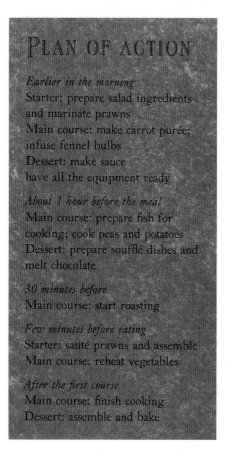

PLAN OF ACTION

Earlier in the morning
Starter: prepare salad ingredients and marinate prawns
Main course: make carrot purée; infuse fennel bulbs
Dessert: make sauce
have all the equipment ready

About 1 hour before the meal
Main course: prepare fish for cooking; cook peas and potatoes
Dessert: prepare soufflé dishes and melt chocolate

30 minutes before
Main course: start roasting

Few minutes before eating
Starter: sauté prawns and assemble
Main course: reheat vegetables

After the first course
Main course: finish cooking
Dessert: assemble and bake

SOPHISTICATED HOT PRAWN SALAD

6 or 9 (depending on size) raw prawns (or jumbo cooked prawns)
1 or 2 garlic cloves, finely chopped
1cm/½in piece of fresh root ginger, peeled and finely chopped
1 unwaxed lime
several sprigs of coriander
¼ tsp hot chilli paste
2 tsp soya sauce
1 tsp anchovy paste
small pinch of five-spice powder
3-4 tbsp groundnut oil
about 2 tsp sesame oil
about 115g/4oz mixed salad leaves, such as oakleaf lettuce, lamb's lettuce, soft lettuce, frisée
1 tbsp pine kernels
2 tsp sesame seeds
sea salt and freshly ground black pepper

Peel the prawns and de-vein them – but leave their tails on.

Put the garlic and ginger in a small bowl. Grate the zest from about half the lime into the bowl. Squeeze the juice from the lime and add 2 teaspoons of it to the bowl. Snip in a few coriander leaves, then stir in the chilli paste, soya sauce, anchovy paste, five-spice powder and 1 tablespoon of groundnut oil. Mix well with a fork, small spoon or whisk.

Sprinkle the prawns generously with sesame oil, then dip them one by one into the spice mixture. Sprinkle any remaining mixture over the prawns and chill for at least 20 minutes.

A few minutes before serving, coarsely shred the salad leaves into a bowl and snip in the remaining coriander leaves. Dress lightly with a sprinkling of lime juice and a little groundnut oil. Season with salt and pepper. Divide between the serving plates.

Heat 1 tablespoon of groundnut oil in a frying pan. Sauté the coated prawns for 5-6 minutes (2–3 minutes if cooked), turning them over once and shaking the pan a few times to cook them evenly. Remove from the pan with a fish slice and arrange on the salad. Sprinkle over any remaining lime juice.

Reduce the heat under the frying pan and add 2 teaspoons of groundnut oil. Heat through, then throw in the pine kernels and sauté for 1 minute. Add the sesame seeds and sauté for a few more seconds. Sprinkle the toasted nuts over the salad and serve at once.

Right *Sophisticated Hot Prawn Salad. Raw Prawns have an inimitable texture but may not be as readily available as cooked prawns. Use very large or jumbo-sized Pacific or Mediterranean prawns and prepare as above, but sauté for only 2-3 minutes.*

36

SEA BASS WITH ROAST FENNEL

1 small sea bass, weighing about
    675g/1 ½lb
6 small fennel bulbs
2 tbsp fennel seeds
2 tbsp Pernod or brandy
about 3 tbsp virgin olive oil
5 tbsp dry white wine
5 tbsp light fish stock (see page 8)
30g/1oz unsalted butter, chilled
sea salt and freshly ground black pepper

Scale and gut the fish thoroughly. Wash it inside and out under cold running water and pat dry with paper towels.

Preheat the oven to 220C/425F/gas7.

Trim the fennel bulbs, removing large fronds and cutting out hard cores, reserving some of the leafy fronds for decorating the fish, if you like. Cut the bulbs in half lengthwise if they are on the large side. Rinse and drain, but do not pat dry.

In a small bowl, sprinkle 1 tablespoon of fennel seeds with 1 tablespoon of the Pernod or brandy and leave to infuse.

Brush a small roasting pan with olive oil. Sprinkle over 2 teaspoons of the remaining fennel seeds. Put the prepared fennel in the pan, brush each bulb all over generously with olive oil and roast for about 20 minutes, turning them over halfway through cooking.

Season the cavity of the fish gener-ously with salt and freshly ground pepper. Spoon the infused fennel seeds and their liquid into the cavity.

Remove the roasting pan from the oven. Moisten the roasted fennel with the wine and stock. Place the fish on top and season it with salt and pepper. Then trickle over a little olive oil. Cover the pan with foil and bake for 10-15 minutes. Remove and reserve the foil and continue cooking the fish for 5 minutes, until the flesh is just opaque.

Preheat the grill to high. Put the reserved foil over the grill pan or rack to retain any juices. Using a fish slice and spatula, carefully transfer the fish from the roasting pan to the foil. Sprinkle with the remaining fennel seeds and Pernod or brandy and grill for a minute or so. Keep hot.

While the fish is under the grill, arrange the fennel on a warmed serving plate and make the sauce: bring the pan juices to the boil on top of the hob, then reduce the heat a little. Cut the chilled butter into 4 pieces and whisk these into the pan, stirring well into the juices. Adjust the seasoning.

Carefully place the sea bass on the serving dish. Add any juices from the foil to the sauce. Using a small sieve or strainer, trickle the sauce over the fish. Garnish with fennel fronds, if wished, and serve as soon as possible.

CARROT AND POTATO PURÉE

350g/12oz waxy potatoes in their skins
225g/8oz carrots
100ml/3 ½fl oz chicken or vegetable stock
45g/1 ½oz butter
2 tbsp milk
2 tbsp double cream
few sprigs of chervil
sea salt and freshly ground black pepper

Bring a saucepan of water to the boil and cook the potatoes in their skins until just done, keeping the heat low to moderate and the water just simmering. Drain and leave to cool for a few minutes. Rinse out the pan.

While the potatoes are cooking, scrape the carrots and cut them into thinnish slices. Bring the stock to a simmer in a saucepan which has a lid and season with a pinch of salt. Add the carrots, cover and cook for 10-15 minutes, or until just tender. Drain, reserving 1-2 tablespoons of the stock. Whizz the carrots with the reserved stock in a blender or food processor.

Skin the cooled potatoes and push them through a vegetable mill. Melt the butter in the rinsed-out pan, add the milk and cream and heat through gently. Then add the puréed potatoes and beat them in not too vigorously. Season. Fold in the puréed carrots and adjust the seasoning, if necessary. Serve hot with a last-minute sprinkling of snipped chervil.

Top Sea Bass with Roast Fennel.

PEAS WITH ALMONDS AND LETTUCE STRIPS

1 tbsp slivered blanched almonds
45g/1 ¹/₂oz butter
¹/₂ small soft lettuce
225g/8oz shelled baby peas (about 400g/
  14oz unshelled) or frozen garden peas
100ml/3 ¹/₂fl oz light stock or water
sea salt and freshly ground black pepper

Season the almonds. In a sauté pan, melt half the butter and sauté the almonds until just golden. Drain well on paper towels.

Wash and coarsely shred the lettuce. Add the rest of the butter to the pan, followed by the peas and lettuce. Season lightly, stir and cover. Cook over a low to moderate heat for 5 minutes, shaking the pan occasionally.

Pour in the liquid and continue cooking until the peas are tender. Adjust the seasoning, drain well and serve sprinkled with the almonds.

If using frozen peas, cook from frozen in stock and then drain. Add the butter to the pan, wilt the lettuce and stir in the peas. Cook for 1 minute.

CHOCOLATE SOUFFLÉED PUDDINGS WITH GINGER SAUCE

100g/3 ¹/₂oz dark bitter chocolate
pinch of ground ginger
grated zest of ¹/₂ unwaxed orange
2 tbsp single cream
2 large eggs, separated
few drops of lemon juice
75g/2 ¹/₂oz caster sugar
unsalted butter, for greasing
icing sugar, for dusting (optional)

FOR THE GINGER SAUCE:
2 pieces of stem ginger in syrup, drained
  but reserving 2 tbsp of the syrup
freshly squeezed juice of ¹/₂ large or 1
  small orange
2 tbsp ginger wine

Butter 3 small soufflé dishes, ramekins or pudding basins with a diameter of about 10cm/4in. Chill for at least 30 minutes.

First prepare the ginger sauce: cut the pieces of ginger into quarters. Whizz them in a food processor, then trickle in the orange juice, ginger wine and reserved syrup. Whizz again and chill until ready to serve.

Break the chocolate into small pieces. Put these in a bowl with 1 teaspoon of water and stand the bowl over a pan of very hot water. Stir until the chocolate has melted, then stir in the ginger and the grated orange zest. If the soufflés are not going to be baked immediately, leave the mixture over hot water and stir occasionally.

Preheat the oven to 180-190C/350-375F/gas4-5. Remove the soufflé dishes from the refrigerator and grease them again with butter.

Using a whisk, work the cream into the chocolate followed by the egg yolks. Whisk the whites with a few drops of lemon juice. When the mixture stiffens, lightly whisk in the sugar. Using a metal spoon, carefully fold the whisked egg whites into the chocolate cream.

Pour or spoon this mixture into the dishes. Bake for about 20 minutes, until well risen and just crusty on the outside. Dust lightly with icing sugar, if liked, and serve immediately.

To eat, break open the top of each soufflé and pour a little ginger sauce into the middle.

MIDSUMMER FEAST

*a cool
light lunch inspired by
Scandinavia*

MENU

FOR 6-8

*Cucumber Salad
Hot Quails' Eggs*

* * *

*Gravad Lax
Sweet Dill Mustard Sauce
Herbed Baby New Potatoes*

* * *

*Spiced Biscuits
Red Fruit Bowl*

40

LET me start with a confession: I have never actually been in Scandinavia for Midsummer . . . I have been there in winter, in spring and in late summer, but never on the feast day my Scandinavian friends tell me so much about. They do seem to spend the rest of the year either reminiscing about or looking forward to their great festival.

The grass is always greener: I like the uncompromising style of Scandinavian cuisine, the ingredients it uses and its clean strong tastes. It excels at combining salt and sweet in a way that may well hark back to medieval times but – to me – is wonderfully exotic and different. The most successful sweet-and-salt combination has to be *gravad lax* or *gravlax*, a splendid way to rediscover salmon. Of course, you can buy marinated salmon ready-made from good supermarkets; but it is fun to prepare, and the end result will be much more interesting. If you find the flavour of dill overwhelming – and it is pretty assertive – use just a tiny bit and make up the quantity with herbs you know you like. A mixture of flat-leaf parsley, tarragon and thyme works very nicely.

To kick off this meal, try the Hot Quails' Eggs on page 106-7. They too are Scandinavian in spirit – a Danish guest chef at the Savoy once showed me how to prepare them at a brunch party. It was an elegant occasion, but he used hens' eggs rather than the miniature models. If I am feeling truly festive, I would also hand out blinis (or small fresh rye bread *tartines*) with salmon eggs, finely chopped red onion, crème fraîche and a touch of lemon juice.

TO DRINK: rather than wine, the occasion calls for tiny chilled glasses of icy Absolut vodka with the appetizers and your favourite lager thereafter.

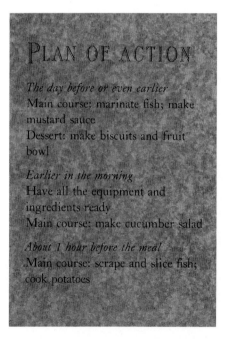

PLAN OF ACTION

The day before or even earlier
Main course: marinate fish; make mustard sauce
Dessert: make biscuits and fruit bowl

Earlier in the morning
Have all the equipment and ingredients ready
Main course: make cucumber salad

About 1 hour before the meal
Main course: scrape and slice fish; cook potatoes

CUCUMBER SALAD

1 large or 2 small firm cucumber(s), very thinly sliced
4-5 tbsp white wine vinegar
about 1-2 tbsp caster sugar
few sprigs each of parsley and tarragon, snipped
sea salt and freshly ground black pepper

Put the cucumber in a large colander and sprinkle liberally with salt. Cover it with a plate, put a weight on it and leave to drain for 1 hour. Rinse off the salt, drain thoroughly and squeeze out any remaining juices.

Bring to the boil about 100ml/3½ fl oz of water with a good pinch of salt and a little freshly ground black pepper. Leave to cool, then season to taste with vinegar and sugar (start with 1 heaped tablespoon of sugar, check the taste and adjust if necessary). Leave the dressing to get completely cold, then pour it over the cucumber and chill for 1 hour.

Sprinkle with finely snipped tarragon and parsley, and adjust the seasoning of the dressing just before serving.

GRAVAD LAX

1.35k/3 ½lb salmon or salmon trout,
*   without the head and cut lengthwise into*
*   2 fillets with the skin left on*
2 ½ tbsp sea salt
3 tbsp caster sugar
2-3 tsp crushed white peppercorns
finely grated zest of ½ unwaxed lemon
1arge bunch of dill fronds and stems,
*   coarsely snipped*
more dill sprigs, to garnish (optional)

TO SERVE:
lemon wedges
buttered thinly sliced brown bread
freshly ground black pepper

Check the fish fillets for small bones
with the palm of the hand and remove
with tweezers. Scrape the skin and dry
the fish with a clean cloth.

Combine the salt, sugar, peppercorns
and grated lemon zest. Rub both sides
of the fillets with this mixture, reserving
a generous tablespoon.

Put a layer of dill in a shallow dish,
then place a fillet skin-side down on the
dill. Sprinkle with dill and cover with
the second fillet, skin-side up. Sprinkle
this with dill and then with the rest of
the spice mixture. Cover with a
weighted plate and chill for 12-36 hours
(the longer the fish marinates, the deeper
the flavour will be). Turn the fish over
halfway through.

To serve, scrape off the spices and
dill and pat the fish dry with a clean tea
towel or paper towels. Cut the fish into
very thin slices, squeeze a little lemon
juice over them and chill for 1 hour.

Garnish the slices of fish with fresh
dill sprigs, if using, and serve with
lemon wedges and black pepper,
buttered brown bread and the Sweet
Dill Mustard Sauce.

Above Quails' eggs are a delicious starter
for a Scandinavian feast.

SWEET DILL
MUSTARD SAUCE

MAKES ABOUT 175ML/6FL OZ

2 tbsp sweet mustard
2 tsp caster sugar
1 tbsp white wine vinegar or lemon juice
6 tbsp groundnut oil
1 tbsp finely snipped dill fronds
1 tbsp finely snipped chives
2 tbsp crème fraîche

In a bowl, combine the mustard, sugar
and vinegar or lemon juice. Whisk in
the oil, a little at a time, until the sauce
thickens. Stir in the chopped herbs
followed by the cream.

Chill until needed. This sauce will
keep for a few days and is delicious with
boiled potatoes – even without salmon.

HERBED BABY
NEW POTATOES

900g/2lb baby new potatoes
15g/ ½oz butter, softened
few sprigs of parsley and small bunch of
*   chives, finely snipped*
sea salt and freshly ground black pepper

Take a large heavy saucepan with a
tight-fitting lid into which you can fit a
steaming basket. Put about 5cm/2in of
water in the pan and bring to the boil.
Arrange the potatoes in an even layer in
the steaming basket and put this over the
boiling water. Cover and steam gently
for 20-25 minutes, depending on the
size of the potatoes, until tender.

Season the potatoes lightly and gently
toss them in butter to make them shine.
Sprinkle with the snipped herbs and
serve hot or warm.

RED FRUIT BOWL

450g/1lb mixed red berries, defrosted if
 frozen
170g/6oz caster sugar, plus extra for
 sprinkling
about 1 tbsp cornflour
2 tbsp crème de cassis, framboise, cherry
 liqueur or other red fruit liqueur
small knob of unsalted butter
45g/1 1/2oz slivered almonds

TO SERVE:
350g/12oz fresh mixed red berries
bowl of crème fraîche

Place the fruit in a saucepan with about
850ml/1½ pt water. Simmer until just
tender and then drain. Push the fruit
through a fine sieve into a bowl. Return
this purée to the pan and bring to the
boil. Then reduce the heat a little and
stir in the sugar.

Mix the cornflour with a little water
and stir this into the purée with the
liqueur. Simmer for 3-5 minutes,
stirring constantly until the mixture
thickens (it should be wobbly rather
than solid). Leave to cool, stirring
occasionally, then pour into a glass bowl
or dish.

Melt the butter in a frying pan and
sauté the almonds in it for 1 minute.
Sprinkle with a little caster sugar and
stir for a minute more. Press with paper
towels to remove excess fat. Scatter the
almonds over the fruit bowl. Leave to
cool and chill for 2 hours, or overnight.

To serve: scatter fresh red berries on
top of the fruit bowl and put on the
table with the Spiced Biscuits and a bowl
of crème fraîche.

SPICED BISCUITS

MAKES ABOUT 20 BISCUITS

250g/8 1/2oz flour, plus extra for flouring
pinch of salt
1/2 tsp baking powder
150g/5 1/2oz icing sugar
1 tbsp light brown sugar
1 scant tsp ground ginger
1/2 tsp ground allspice
1/2 tsp ground cinnamon
very small dusting of black pepper
1/2 tsp vanilla essence
200g/7oz unsalted butter, diced, plus extra
 for greasing

TO SERVE:
icing sugar
ground ginger
ground cinnamon

In a food processor, whizz together the
flour, salt, baking powder, sugars and
spices. Then whizz in the vanilla essence
and the diced butter, followed by 1
tablespoon of water.

Remove the resulting dough from the
bowl (it will be a little sticky) and work
it with the palm of the hands for a
couple of minutes. Wrap and chill for
1-2 hours.

Preheat the oven to 190C/375F/gas5
and lightly grease 2 baking sheets.

Roll out the dough to a thickness of
about 6mm/¼in. Cut it into rounds
with a floured 6.5cm/2½in pastry
cutter. Make some of the rounds into
crescent shapes by using the cutter set in
from the edge.

Arrange the rounds and crescents a
little apart on the baking sheets and bake
for about 12 minutes until golden and
firm. Occasionally turn the baking sheets
during baking (the crescents will be
ready a little earlier than the round
biscuits). Using a palette knife, transfer
the baked biscuits to a wire rack and
leave them to cool.

When completely cold, store in an
airtight container. Serve the biscuits
dusted with a little icing sugar mixed
with a pinch of ground ginger and a
touch of cinnamon.

Left *Crème fraîche with a redcurrant
sprig.*

HAPPY HOMECOMING

an easy lunch to return to

MENU

FOR 6-8

Asparagus with Paprika Butter

* * *

*Caucasian Lamb
Bulghar Pilaf*

* * *

Pan-fried Pears

46

THIS is a casual lunch inspired by a wonderful meal I had at the home of a friend and neighbour, where everybody joined in the cooking. The idea is that you make the casserole before you leave home, go out and enjoy yourself and then come back with your guests for a late lunch. If people offer to give a hand with the preparations, all well and good – there are plenty of tasks that can be delegated.

I have tried using various cuts of lamb for the main course and have come to the conclusion that chunky lamb steaks work best. Like all honest casseroles, this one is nothing if not tolerant. There's no need to worry about the timing and, if you are in a hurry, you can cut corners by not bothering to peel the vegetables. If you are really pushed, don't even sauté the aubergines: the end result will be a little less subtle but still tenderly fragrant.

VEGETARIAN OPTION: using exactly the same method, replace the lamb with large flat mushrooms. These will absorb the other flavours very nicely and keep their pleasing texture.

TO DRINK: remember to chill a bottle of 'méthode traditionnelle' sparkling wine before you go out. Give your helpers a glass of Red Fizz (see page 18) to encourage them to work hard. With the lamb, I would suggest drinking a Shiraz Cabernet Sauvignon, and it will also be fine with the dessert.

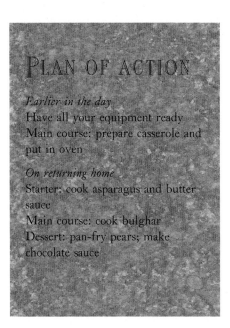

PLAN OF ACTION

Earlier in the day
Have all your equipment ready
Main course: prepare casserole and put in oven

On returning home
Starter: cook asparagus and butter sauce
Main course: cook bulghar
Dessert: pan-fry pears; make chocolate sauce

ASPARAGUS WITH PAPRIKA BUTTER

1k/2 ¼lb sprue asparagus
140g/5oz unsalted butter
1 tsp lemon juice
1large pinch of paprika
sea salt
bread, to serve

In a large sauté pan, bring about 5cm/2in water to the boil with a generous pinch of salt.

Wash the asparagus and cut off the tough ends, trimming the asparagus to about 10cm/4in lengths.

Drop the stalks into the pan, bring back to the boil and simmer for 4-5 minutes until the asparagus stalks are just tender (they will collapse if over-cooked).

Lift the stalks out of the water with a fish slice or skimmer. Leave to drain and cool on a folded clean tea towel or several layers of paper towels.

Meanwhile, cut the butter into pieces and heat gently in a small heavy sauce-pan until melted. (If time allows, or if you are not going to use it immediately, clarify the butter: cook the melted butter until it starts to separate, then strain into a cup, discarding the sediment. Rinse out the pan, wipe dry and pour the clarified butter back in.) Stir in the lemon juice and paprika.

Fan out the asparagus stalks on individual plates and dribble the hot paprika butter over the tips. Serve with bread, large napkins and, ideally, with finger bowls.

CAUCASIAN LAMB

6 large lamb leg steaks
2 aubergines
1 green or yellow sweet pepper
6 tomatoes
1 ½ Spanish onions
1 apple
12 dried apricots and/or prunes, pre-
  soaked if necessary
4 spring onions
4-6 tbsp olive oil, plus extra for greasing
½ tsp ground cinnamon
½ tsp ground cloves
1 tsp ground cumin
1 tsp ground coriander
2 stalks of lemon grass
3 garlic cloves
sea salt and freshly ground black pepper
Greek-style yogurt, to serve

Trim and discard as much visible fat
from the lamb as possible and cut each
steak into 2 pieces.

Prepare the vegetables and fruit. Cut
the aubergines on the slant into thin
slices. Put these in a colander, sprinkle
with salt and leave to stand for 30
minutes.

Blanch the pepper in boiling water
for about 3-5 minutes, turning it over a
few times so that all sides are immersed
for a while, then fish it out. Leave until
cool enough to handle and then peel off
the skin. Cut off and discard the core
and seeds, then cut the flesh into strips.

In the same boiling water, blanch the
tomatoes for 1 minute. Then peel and
halve them. Slice the onions thinly.
Core, peel and chop the apple. Halve
the apricots and/or prunes. Trim the
spring onions.

Preheat the oven to 160C/325F/gas3
and lightly oil an ovenproof casserole
dish with olive oil.

Spread half the tomatoes over the base
of the dish. Top with half the pepper
and half the onion, then add half the
fruit.

Dribble a good tablespoon of olive oil
into a large frying-pan. Heat this
through and sauté the lamb for a couple
of minutes on each side, in batches, if
necessary. Season with salt and pepper,
sprinkle with the ground spices and cook
for 1 or 2 more minutes, stirring
frequently.

Spoon the spiced and sautéed lamb
over the vegetables and fruit in the
casserole. Finely cut the central core of
each lemon grass stalk and sprinkle it
over the lamb pieces. Cut the garlic
cloves in half and dot them over the
dish. Tuck in the spring onions. Cover
with the rest of the tomatoes, pepper,
onion, and fruit.

Rinse the aubergine slices and pat
them dry firmly with paper towels. Heat
3 tablespoons of oil in the frying-pan
and gently sauté the aubergines in
batches, without overlapping the slices,
until just golden. Cook the rest
carefully, keeping the heat low and
adding a little extra oil when necessary.
Arrange the sautéed aubergines over the
vegetables and fruit.

Cover the casserole tightly – using a
layer of foil if the lid of your casserole
does not fit closely enough – and cook in
the oven for about 1½ hours, until the
meat and vegetables are cooked through
and tender. Adjust seasoning, if
necessary. Serve straight from the
casserole, accompanied by a bowl of
Greek-style yogurt.

BULGHAR PILAF

550g/1 ¼lb bulghar (cracked wheat)
about 575ml/1pt chicken or vegetable stock
30g/1oz butter
sea salt and freshly ground black pepper
few sprigs of flat-leaf parsley, to serve
  (optional)

Using a measuring jug, determine the
volume of the bulghar. In a saucepan,
bring to the boil the same volume of
stock and season it lightly with salt.

Pour in the bulghar and season with
pepper. Cover and simmer over a low
heat for 10-15 minutes, until the grains
are tender and the stock absorbed.

Stir in the butter, cover again and
leave to stand for 10-15 minutes before
serving. If you like, snip a little parsley
over the dish before serving.

PAN-FRIED PEARS

1k/2 ¼lb ripe pears
125g/4 ½oz unsalted butter
150g/5 ½oz caster sugar
1 tbsp Poire Williams brandy (optional)
vanilla ice-cream, to serve

FOR THE CHOCOLATE SAUCE:
150g/5 ½oz bitter chocolate
3 tbsp single cream
icing sugar to taste (optional)

Quarter, core and peel the pears.

In a large heavy frying-pan, melt three-quarters of the butter over a low heat. Sprinkle in three-quarters of the sugar, swirling it around so that the whole pan is coated.

Take the pan off the heat. Place the pear quarters in the pan, return to a moderate heat and cook for 10 minutes. Turn over the pieces of pear, dot with the rest of the butter and sprinkle with the rest of the sugar. Cook over a low heat for a further 10-15 minutes until the pears are golden and caramelized. Keep warm.

While the pears are cooking, make the chocolate sauce: break the chocolate into small pieces and combine these with 2 tablespoons of water in a small heavy-based saucepan. Melt over a minimal heat, stirring occasionally. Just before serving, stir in the cream and sweeten with a little icing sugar, if necessary.

If you like, sprinkle the cooked pears with a little liqueur at the last minute. Serve with the ice-cream and the chocolate sauce in a separate bowl.

Left Pan-fried Pears. This dessert was originally intended as a variation on Tarte Tatin. The caramelized pears proved so delicious that my helpers and tasters decided no pastry was needed.

PORTABLE FEAST

finger-food for family picnics

MENU

FOR 5 OR MORE

Pan Bagna
Asperges Gourmandes

* * *

Tortilla Habershon
Glazed Chicken Drumsticks

* * *

Fresh Summer Fruit with Custard
Cream Dip

52

To my mind picnics have to strike a happy balance – on the one hand I hate them to be too 'refined' (perhaps 'refayned' would be a more appropriate spelling for my particular phobia). On the other, I like my food far too much to have a dull meal just because it happens to be a picnic.

You will need neither knives nor forks to enjoy my portable feast. Asparagus tastes much better eaten with your hands anyway and chicken drumsticks were devised to be hand-held, as were strawberries with their little stalks. For the tortilla recipe I must thank my friend Alison Habershon, who perfected it over the years while living in Spain. It was her family's favourite picnic fare and their guests, myself included, still wolf it down happily at Habershon parties.

The baked drumsticks are served cold, but also taste pretty good hot. I have allowed about 2 tablespoons of marinade for each drumstick. For a less casual occasion, I use the same (total) amount of marinade to coat 2-3 leg portions. Cook for 1¼-1½ hours and leave to settle in the switched-off oven for 15 minutes before serving on individual plates with a well-dressed mixed leaf salad. This is so appealing that I find even reluctant leaf-eaters will devour this particular 'salady' meal.

Fruit is the best dessert for picnics. Serve the most luscious possible combination of the fresh fruits of the season. I love to combine them with a little chilled rich creamy custard but crème fraîche with a little sugar is a possible alternative, if you don't feel like making custard.

TO DRINK: a bottle of well-made dry rosé for the wine drinkers, mineral water for all, plus cans of lager and coke . . . what really matters is to have plenty of chilled drinks at hand as having a picnic is thirsty work.

PLAN OF ACTION

The day before
Make ice cubes and chill drinks
Main course: marinate drumsticks
Dessert: make custard

Earlier in the morning
Main course: bake drumsticks (could be done the day before if more convenient); make tortilla
Starters: prepare Pan Bagna; cook asparagus; make dressing

Just before leaving
Assemble picnic equipment
Main course: wrap tortilla and drumsticks
Dessert: prepare and arrange fruit

TORTILLA HABERSHON

about 575ml/1pt mixed sunflower oil and olive oil
675g/1 ½lb good-quality waxy potatoes, peeled and sliced into 6mm/¼in chunks
2 Spanish onions, thinly sliced
7 large eggs
2 garlic cloves, crushed (optional)
few sprigs of flat-leaf parsley (optional)
few thin strips of charred and peeled red pepper (optional: see page 29)
sea salt and freshly ground black pepper
chopped flat-leaf parsley, to garnish (optional)
tomato ketchup, to serve

Pour just enough of the oil mixture into a 28cm/11in cast-iron or non-stick frying pan so that it is about one-third full. Heat the oil and gently sauté half the potatoes, keeping an eye on the pan at all times and turning the potatoes over several times during cooking.

When they are cooked through and some are golden and crisp, remove them from the pan using a slotted spoon. Drain them well on paper towels. Repeat with the second batch.

Once all the potatoes are cooked, reduce the heat and sauté the onions until soft and translucent. Drain well. Pat both potatoes and onions with paper towels to remove any surplus oil.

Beat the eggs in a large bowl. Add the garlic, if using, and season to taste with salt and pepper. Add the drained potatoes and onion, together with the parsley and charred red pepper, if using. Stir gently.

Strain most of the oil from the pan into a bowl or jug, just leaving a good coating in the pan. Heat this until very hot, then pour in the egg mixture. Allow the bottom to set, then reduce the heat and continue cooking, shaking the pan to prevent the omelette from sticking. Cook gently until the omelette is three-quarters set.

Place a serving plate or board larger than the pan on top of it. Using a kitchen glove or a thick cloth, with one hand grab the handle as close as possible to where it joins the pan to give more control. Keeping the plate or board firmly against the pan with the other hand, (take a deep breath and) turn the pan and plate or board upside down. The omelette should safely land on the plate or board.

Dribble a little more of the oil into the pan and turn up the heat. Now slide the omelette back into the pan. Cook over a high heat for a couple of minutes until the other side is set. Then reduce the heat and continue cooking until the whole thing is firm.

Using the same method as earlier, transfer the omelette to a large serving plate. Cover with a plate of the same size. Wrap tightly in layers of newspaper to keep warm.

Serve cut into squares, garnished with chopped parsley, if wished. Supply wooden cocktail sticks to spear the tortilla squares and serve with lots of tomato ketchup.

GLAZED CHICKEN DRUMSTICKS

10 chicken drumsticks
sea salt and freshly ground black pepper

FOR THE SPICY MARINADE:
2 large juicy garlic cloves, crushed
4 tbsp oil
6 tbsp orange juice
1 tbsp grated peeled fresh root ginger
1 tsp chilli paste or powder
1 tbsp horseradish mustard or 2 tsp strong
*   mustard mixed with 1 tsp grated*
*   horseradish*
2 tbsp soya sauce
2 tsp finely grated zest from an unwaxed
*   lime or lemon*
scant 1 tbsp clear honey
several drops of Worcestershire sauce

FOR THE HERB MARINADE:
2-3 large juicy garlic cloves, crushed
4 tbsp olive oil
1 tbsp French mustard
1 tbsp Mascarpone cheese, cream cheese or
*   thick cream*
6 tbsp white wine
1 tsp caster sugar
several sprigs each of flat-leaf parsley and
*   thyme leaves, snipped*
1-2 tsp dried oregano
snipped leaves from a sprig of rosemary, or
*   1 tsp dried rosemary*
1 tsp finely grated zest from an unwaxed
*   orange or lemon*
few drops of Tabasco
few drops of Worcestershire sauce

Using a sharp knife, deeply score the chicken drumsticks in several places.

Combine the ingredients for each marinade in a separate bowl. Season each to taste.

Swirl half of the drumsticks in the spicy marinade until well coated, then put them in a single layer in a flameproof dish. Spoon the rest of the marinade over the handle ends of the drumsticks. Repeat with the remaining drumsticks and the other marinade in a separate dish. Cover and marinate in the refrigerator for at least 2 hours, or preferably overnight.

Preheat the oven to 180C/350F/gas4.

Bake the drumsticks for 50-60 minutes until cooked through. Leave to settle in the switched-off oven for 15 minutes. Remove from the oven and allow to cool, then chill until needed.

ASPERGES GOURMANDES

1k/2 ¼lb thinnish green or purple
  asparagus
sea salt and freshly ground black pepper

FOR THE VINAIGRETTE
GOURMANDE:
1 large egg, hard-boiled
1 tbsp wine vinegar
100ml/3 ½fl oz groundnut or sunflower oil
small bunch of chives, finely snipped
few sprigs of flat-leaf parsley, finely snipped

Put about 5cm/2in water in a large sauté
pan with a generous pinch of salt and
bring to the boil.

Wash the asparagus. Cut off the
tough ends, trimming the asparagus to
no more than about 10cm/4in lengths.

Drop the asparagus stalks into the
pan. Bring back to the boil and simmer
for 5-10 minutes, depending on size,
until the asparagus stalks are just cooked
but still have some crunch – they will be
easier to hold and travel better.

Lift the asparagus out of the water
with a fish slice or skimmer. Empty the
pan, carefully put the asparagus back in
the pan and leave to dry for 30 seconds.
Take out and leave to get cold on a
folded clean tea towel or several layers
of paper towels.

Make the vinaigrette: grate the egg
into a screw-top jar (if you are a
perfectionist, push the grated egg
through a fine sieve into the jar). Add
the vinegar and oil, stir well and season
generously with salt and pepper. Chill
until ready to go on the picnic.

Stir the snipped herbs into the
vinaigrette just before serving or leaving
for the picnic.

Left Ready to go: Pan Bagna, dressed
asparagus and tortilla.

PAN BAGNA

MAKES 4

4 baps or soft large round rolls
1 garlic clove, halved
about 3 tbsp good-quality olive oil
2 large ripe tomatoes
1 sweet white onion or white parts of 3
  large spring onions, thinly sliced
8-12 black olives, pitted and halved
200g/7oz canned flaked tuna in brine,
  drained (optional)
115g/4oz cooked French green beans
few lettuce leaves, shredded
small pinch of dried thyme
small pinch of dried oregano
sea salt and freshly ground black pepper

Cut each bap or roll in half and rub the
insides with the cut sides of the garlic.
Sprinkle the base with olive oil.

Arrange a few slices of tomato and
some onion or spring onion on the oiled
surface. Add some black olives and a
little tuna, if using. Season. Top with
green beans and lettuce leaves. Sprinkle
with the herbs, season again and dribble
just a little more olive oil over the
leaves.

Cover with the other half of the bap
or roll, press together and wrap in paper
towels and foil.

Leave to settle for at least 30 minutes
before eating.

FRESH SUMMER FRUIT WITH CUSTARD CREAM DIP

300ml/ ½ pt full-fat milk, infused with a
  vanilla pod for a few hours
2 egg yolks
75g/2 ½ oz caster sugar
1 tbsp kirsch
3 tbsp double cream
about 900g/2lb fresh strawberries and
  other summer fruit, to serve

Gently heat the milk and then remove
the vanilla pod.

In a heavy-based saucepan, whisk the
egg yolks with the sugar until smooth
and pale. Put the pan over a low heat
and gradually pour in the hot milk,
stirring well with a wooden spoon.

Bring the mixture almost to the boil
and keep stirring until the custard is
thick enough to coat the back of the
spoon. Take the pan off the heat
occasionally to keep the cooking
temperature under control – it should
never be allowed to boil.

Strain the custard through a fine sieve
into a bowl. Stir in the kirsch and
cream. Allow to cool, stirring
occasionally, and then chill until ready
to use.

Serve as a dip with an assortment of
summer fruit.

*Left The best of the summer fruit season is
all too brief, so indulge yourself while you
can.*

POSTPONED POUSSINS

*a small late lunch on
a winter afternoon*

MENU

FOR 4

*Smoked Salmon Stars
with Paprika Cream Cheese*

* * *

*Poussins Done Like Game Birds
Herbed Lentils
Wilted Spinach, Lettuce
and Radicchio*

FIRST served this lunch on one of those rare bright winter's days when the sun actually felt warm for a while. Too good to miss! The smoked salmon starter was in the refrigerator . . . the lentils nearly cooked . . . so I basted the two-thirds-cooked poussins, covered them with foil and left them for a good long while in a very low oven while we went out to enjoy the day. By the time we came back at dusk the poussins were perfectly tender and still very moist.

Perhaps because of the disjointed timetable that particular afternoon, we did not have a 'proper' dessert, but feasted on farmhouse cheeses with wheaten biscuits. I still think they round off this meal rather nicely.

SHOPPING: you may have to hunt around a little to find good small lentils. Look out for bluey-green *lentilles du Puy* from France. If you are near an Italian delicatessen, ask if they happen to have little brown Castelluccio lentils from Umbria.

TO DRINK: kir royale, made with dry Sparkling Saumur, when you come in from your walk. Finish the bottle, perhaps without cassis, with the salmon starter. The rest is up to you. I know that the first time I had this meal we drank some Clairet, a very light red wine a friend had brought back from Bordeaux – the name of which apparently gave rise to the English term 'claret'.

PLAN OF ACTION

Earlier in the day
Assemble equipment and have ingredients ready
Main course: coat poussins; cook lentils
Starter: assemble and chill

About 1 ½ hours before the meal
Main course: start cooking
Dessert: prepare cheese board

Few minutes before eating
Main course: cook spinach
Starter: sprinkle with salmon eggs and finish off

SMOKED SALMON STARS WITH PAPRIKA CREAM CHEESE

about 225g/8oz thinly sliced smoked
 salmon
100g/3 ¹/₂oz cream cheese
1 tbsp lemon juice
paprika
small bunch of chives
sea salt and freshly ground black pepper

TO SERVE:
12 very thin lemon slices
55g/2oz salmon eggs
hot blinis, thin slices of toast or sesame
 bread

Cut each slice of salmon in half. Fold
the pieces into triangles and arrange the
triangles on top of one another in the
centre of each plate, with their tips
pointing outwards and at an angle to
each other so that they form a star shape.

Whisk the cream cheese with the
lemon juice and a good sprinkling of
paprika. Snip in some chives and season
generously with salt and pepper.

Heap a little mound of paprika cream
cheese in the centre of each salmon star.
Cut each of the lemon slices a little in
from the edge towards the centre on
either side, but leaving it still joined in
the middle. Then twist to make a
butterfly. Arrange three lemon
butterflies on each plate around the
smoked salmon. Chill until needed.

Just before serving, sprinkle some
salmon eggs over each and snip over
some more chives. Season again with a
touch of paprika and pepper. Serve with
hot blinis, toast or sesame bread.

HERBED LENTILS

350g/12oz good-quality small lentils, such
 as the blue-green lentils from Le Puy
1 tbsp oil
1 Spanish onion, finely chopped
1 garlic clove, crushed
about 850ml/1 ¹/₂pt light chicken stock
 or water
few sprigs of parsley
¹/₂ tsp dried rubbed sage
15g/ ¹/₂oz butter
sea salt and freshly ground black pepper

Rinse the lentils and drain them well.

In a heavy-based saucepan, heat the
oil. Add the onion and sauté it for a few
minutes over a low heat, stirring
occasionally.

When the onion is a little softened,
stir in the garlic, followed by the lentils.
Generously cover with stock or water
(there should be about 2.5cm/1in of
liquid above the lentils) and bring back
to a simmer. Add the parsley and sage.
Season lightly, cover and simmer over a
fairly low heat for 30-40 minutes, until
the lentils are tender but not soft. Check
the cooking occasionally and stir the
lentils from time to time (you may need
to add a tablespoon or two of extra
liquid if they look a little dry).

Just before serving, drain off any
excess liquid (it will be good for soup or
stock) and discard the parsley. Stir in
the butter and adjust the seasoning.
Serve sprinkled with the reserved bacon
from the poussins.

WILTED SPINACH, LETTUCE AND RADICCHIO

550g/1 ¹/₄lb young spinach
1 soft lettuce
1 small head of radicchio
¹/₂ garlic clove
pinch of freshly grated nutmeg
30g/1oz butter
sea salt and freshly ground black pepper
groundnut oil, for greasing

Wash the spinach in plenty of cold
water. Drain, but do not pat dry.
Remove the stalks from the centres of
the leaves. Wash and drain the lettuce
and radicchio. Shred any leaf that seems
too large.

Brush a sauté pan with a little
groundnut oil, then rub with the cut
side of the garlic. Heat the pan through
and, when it is hot, add the spinach.
Cover and cook for 3 minutes over a
moderately high heat, shaking the pan
occasionally.

Stir in the lettuce and radicchio, cover
and cook for 2 minutes. Season with
salt, pepper and a little grated nutmeg.
Stir in the butter and serve.

POUSSINS DONE
LIKE GAME BIRDS

4 small oven-ready poussins
about 115g/4oz butter, softened
½ tsp juniper berries
1 ½ tsp mixed pepper berries, coarsely
*   ground*
½ tsp paprika
½ tsp dried sage
3 sprigs of fresh thyme, snipped, or 1 tsp
*   dried thyme*
1 ½ tbsp oil
150ml/ ¼pt white wine
4 thin slices of good-quality smoked streaky
*   bacon, halved across*
salt and freshly ground black pepper
small bunch of fresh watercress, to serve
*   (optional)*

A few hours before starting the cooking, wipe the poussins inside and out with a clean wet cloth. Put three-quarters of the butter, the berries, paprika, sage and thyme together with a tablespoon of cold water in a food processor and whizz them well. Coat the poussins with this flavoured butter and put a knob of it inside each bird. Leave them to rest in a cool place.

Preheat the oven to 200C/400F/gas6.

In a large flameproof casserole big enough to take the poussins side by side, heat the oil with the rest of the butter and brown the poussins evenly over a moderate heat. Turn the poussins breast side down. Season with salt and pepper and pour in the wine. Return to a simmer and transfer to the oven.

Roast for about 20 minutes, then turn the poussins so their breast sides are uppermost and cover each with two bacon pieces. Cook for another 15 minutes, then remove and reserve the bacon. Baste the birds with cooking juices and lower the heat to 180C/ 350F/gas4. Roast for another 30 minutes, basting once or twice. Leave the poussins to settle in the switched-off warm oven for 10 minutes before serving.

Serve the poussins with the lentils and a bunch of fresh watercress, if using, in the centre of the serving dish. Strain the cooking juices into a warmed sauce boat, adjust the seasoning, then dribble a little sauce over the poussins to moisten them. Snip the reserved bacon over the lentils at the last minute.

Right Lentils and poultry make a great combination. For very hungry guests, try serving Mashed Potatoes (see page 83) as an accompaniment.

FILLING THE GENERATION GAP

*an impressive meal to please
all the family*

MENU

FOR 6-8

*Roast Salmon
Steam-poached Green Vegetables
Pasta and Roast Garlic with
Wilting Sweet Tomatoes*

* * *

Fresh Fruit Trifle

A WHOLE salmon makes a good centre-piece for a family party. It's a safe bet for most palates and it looks impressive. I particularly like it roasted and served with a robust red-wine sauce and pasta.

Sunday being a day of rest and harmony, we had the usual friendly bicker last time I put roast salmon on the table. I had accompanied it with boiled new potatoes to please a pasta-hating senior relative whose birthday we were celebrating. What's more – also in an effort to be extra nice to the said new octogenarian, I had peeled the wretched potatoes. Cooking times came up again, naturally, since I like my salmon moist but not sticky pink. In addition, to my surprise, my brother-in-law, the gastro-enterologist, teased me about the delicious charred skin, 'So you leave on the salmon skin, but you peel potatoes, eh, Marie-Pierre . . .' They were very lucky that the trifle was already in the refrigerator. I went on strike for the rest of the day.

VEGETARIAN OPTION: this meat-free meal can easily be stretched with extra pasta and vegetables to feed hungry vegetarians. Have plenty of good cheese and a grater at their disposal.

SHOPPING: heads of garlic for roasting need to be very fresh and juicy. If the skin looks a little papery, cover the heads with cold water and boil them for 5 minutes. Then rinse them well and pat dry. If you are not entirely sure of the garlic, open a clove or two: if there is even a tiny greenish sprout in the middle – sorry, forget about roasting this time. Instead, take these sprouts out of a couple of cloves with the tip of a small sharp knife and crush the cloves. Combine this with the herbs and sprinkle over the tomatoes.

TO DRINK: I recommend a lightly chilled young Bourgueil. If some of your guests prefer white, however, this dish will easily accommodate a Chardonnay despite the red wine sauce.

PLAN OF ACTION

The day before
Dessert: make and chill trifle (except cream topping)

Earlier in the morning
Have ready all equipment and ingredients
Dessert: whisk cream and add to trifle, then chill
Main course: start sauce

About 1 ½ hours before the meal
Main course: prepare salmon; roast garlic and tomatoes, keep warm

About 1 hour before
Main course: start roasting salmon

About 30 minutes before
Main course: start vegetables; heat water for pasta

Just before eating
Main course: grill salmon and finish off sauce; reheat garlic

Roast salmon

1 small salmon or salmon trout, weighing
    about 1.35-1.5k/3-3 ½lb, cleaned and
    gutted
1 tbsp light olive oil, plus more for
    greasing
3 spring onions
several sprigs each of thyme and flat-leaf
    parsley
75g/2 ½oz unsalted butter, softened
few strips of zest from an unwaxed orange
2 tsp coarse-grain mustard
pinch of paprika
100ml/3 ½fl oz orange juice
sea salt and freshly ground black pepper
wedges of unwaxed orange, to serve
    (optional)

FOR THE SAUCE:
350ml/12fl oz fish or chicken stock
200ml/7fl oz soft fruity red wine
few sprigs of thyme
few strips of zest from an unwaxed orange
pinch of paprika
small pinch of cayenne pepper
45g/1 ½oz chilled unsalted butter, cut
    into pieces

First start the sauce: in a heavy-based
saucepan, combine the stock with the red
wine. Add the thyme and orange zest,
season with a pinch of paprika, a touch
of cayenne, some sea salt and freshly
ground black pepper. Bring to a
bubbling boil, then reduce the heat and
simmer until the liquid is reduced by
half. Adjust the seasoning and keep hot
or leave until needed.

Preheat the oven to 160C/325F/gas3.

Clean and gut the salmon. Generously
oil a large double thickness sheet of foil.

Snip the spring onions and a few
sprigs of thyme and parsley, scattering
them down the centre of the greased
foil. In a small bowl, combine 2
tablespoons of soft butter with the oil,
grated orange zest, mustard, a pinch of
paprika and a good seasoning of salt and
pepper. Snip in some thyme and
parsley. Dribble a little of this mixture
inside the salmon and brush the outside
liberally with the rest.

Place the salmon in the centre of the
foil on top of the herbs and spring
onions. Pour over half the orange juice
and wrap up in a loose parcel, pinching
the edges tightly together.

Bake for about 40-45 minutes. Using
a sharp knife, check that the flesh is just
coming off the bones – if not, bake for
another 5-10 minutes, unless you prefer
your salmon slightly underdone. Turn
off the heat and allow the salmon to rest
in the hot oven for 10 minutes or so.

Preheat the grill to high.

Remove the salmon from the oven,
pour the juices and bits from the foil
into the sauce. Dot the salmon with the
rest of the butter, sprinkle it with the
rest of the orange juice and grill on the
foil for a few minutes until the skin on
top is nicely charred.

Meanwhile, turn on the heat under
the pan of sauce and bring it to a
simmer. Whisk in the chilled butter,
one piece at a time. Add in any juices
from the foil after grilling and pour the
sauce through a fine sieve into a warmed
sauce boat. Adjust the seasoning, if
necessary.

Put the salmon on a warmed serving
dish. Snip over the remaining parsley
and serve at once with orange wedges, if
using, accompanied by the sauce.

Steam-poached green vegetables

350g/12oz baby broad beans, shelled and
    podded
3 baby leeks, trimmed and cut into 2.5cm/
    1in pieces
225g/8oz young garden peas, shelled
225g/8oz mange-tout peas, topped, tailed
    and halved crosswise
few lettuce leaves, rolled and snipped into
    strips
1 tbsp light olive oil
few drops of lemon juice
sea salt and freshly ground black pepper

Bring a kettle full of water to the boil.
Put the broad beans in a large sauté pan
and add just enough of the boiling water
to cover. Season lightly with salt and
bring back to a gentle boil. Cover and
simmer for 2 minutes.

Throw in the leeks, cover and bring
back to the boil. After 1 more minute,
add the peas with a little more boiling
water to cover and a sprinkling of salt.
Cover and boil for 1 minute. Then add
the mange-tout, cover and boil for 1-2
minutes, adding the lettuce for the last
30 seconds of that time. Drain well.

Return the drained vegetables to the
pan, sprinkle with the olive oil and
lemon juice, season and serve.

PASTA AND ROAST GARLIC WITH WILTING SWEET TOMATOES

2 heads of very fresh large-cloved garlic
  (or the large cloves from 2 heads of
  more mature garlic), blanched
350g/12oz ripe but firm small tomatoes or
  large cherry tomatoes
1 tsp balsamic vinegar
2 tsp sugar
1/2 tsp dried sweet savory
1 tsp dried marjoram
400g/14oz dried fettucine or tagliatelle
several sprigs of flat-leaf parsley, finely
  snipped
sea salt and freshly ground black pepper
olive oil, for greasing and sprinkling

Preheat the oven to 160C/325F/gas3. Lightly oil a small roasting or pastry pan and the heads of garlic or the individual cloves. Roast these in the pan near the top of the oven for about 40 minutes until soft.

Once the garlic is in the oven, lightly oil a second small pan. Put the tomatoes in this pan. Sprinkle lightly with olive oil, balsamic vinegar, sugar and herbs. Season with salt and pepper, put in the oven and roast for about 30 minutes.

Leave the roast garlic to cool a little, then squeeze the cloves between thumb and index finger to extract the creamy flesh. Return this to the pan, sprinkle with a little more olive oil and season lightly with salt and pepper. Stir over a moderate heat until mushy and golden brown.

While the garlic and tomatoes are in the oven, cook the pasta until tender in plenty of boiling salted water to which a good dash of olive oil has been added.

Drain the pasta and tip it into a warmed serving bowl. Stir in the parsley, garlic and the juices from the pan. If it looks too dry, sprinkle over a little more olive oil.

Season generously with black pepper and serve at once. Serve the tomatoes separately, warm rather than piping hot.

Left *All on the table: Roast Salmon, Steam-poached Green Vegetables, Pasta and Roast Garlic, Wilting Sweet Tomatoes and Fresh Fruit Trifle with extra fresh fruit.*

70

FRESH FRUIT TRIFLE

*at least 24 savoiardi biscuits, biscuits à la
    cuiller or good sponge fingers*
5 tbsp white rum (or more to taste)
*450g/1lb mixed ripe plums, nectarines and
    apricots*
about 3 tbsp icing sugar
*finely grated zest and juice of a large ripe
    unwaxed orange*
*100g/3 ½oz grilled or roasted slivered
    almonds*
*500ml/16fl oz crème fraîche, double cream
    or Mascarpone cheese*
few mint or angelica leaves

Line the bottom of a large glass bowl
with the biscuits. Moisten them liberally
with the rum mixed with 100ml/3½
fl oz water.

Bring a kettle of water to the boil. In
a bowl, cover the mixed fruit with the
boiling water and leave for 1 minute.
Drain, reserving about 6 tablespoons of
the liquid in a small saucepan.

Skin and stone the fruit as necessary
and cut the flesh into chunks, reserving
the juices and adding these to the
reserved soaking liquid. Sprinkle a little
icing sugar over this fruit liquid, then
stir in half the grated orange zest and 2
tablespoons of the orange juice. (For a
very grown-up trifle, replace half the
orange juice with some orange liqueur.)
Bring to the boil, reduce the heat and
simmer for a minute or two.

Sprinkle a good layer of slivered
almonds over the moistened biscuits.
Cover with the pieces of fruit, then
scatter over another layer of slivered
almonds, reserving a few for the
topping. Dribble the light fruit syrup
over the top. Chill for at least 1 hour,
or overnight if possible.

Whisk the crème fraîche with the rest
of the orange zest and orange juice.
Sweeten to taste with icing sugar. Spoon
this over the almonds and chill for at
least 2 hours.

Scatter with leaves and slivered
almonds just before serving.

Right *Made with plums, apricots and
nectarines, toasted almonds and orange-
flavoured thick cream, this is the simplest
and freshest tasting of trifles.*

FIELD AND FOREST

a flavourful autumn menu

MENU

FOR 4

Mushroom Fricassée

* * *

*Venison Stroganoff
with Forcemeat Balls
Buttered Caraway Noodles
Red Cabbage Hash*

* * *

Queen of Puddings

A MESS of mushrooms is a great way to begin a meal. To my mind a mushroom worth its salt (and pepper and butter) is much too good to eat as a side-dish. A reliable way to do mushrooms justice is to cook them in stages, using a heavy sauté pan. The idea is first to sweat them as this allows them to shed some of their high moisture content. Then allow the worthy fungi to rest and recuperate a while on paper towels. When you then return them to the pan – this time with butter and over a bolder heat – they will be ready to give their full fragrance . . . their outsides just a little seized and their flesh still tender.

If you are using wild mushrooms – and I hope you will be a little extravagant in your choice – add them to their blander cousins towards the end of the sweating process (they only need a minute in the pan at this stage). Start cooking the oyster mushrooms first, as they are resilient little beasts.

Making Venison Stroganoff in a wok may sound like the height of eclecticism, but it works extremely well. Further proof of my (occasional) native thrift, moreover, it is a sensible way to prepare this expensive meat.

Queen of Puddings is one of my favourite English desserts, mellow, sweet nursery food at its most irresistible. The only snag is that it is best straight from the oven and will involve you – the Cook – in a little work while everybody is at table.

TO DRINK: a claret – or a wine made in the style of claret – is called for.

PLAN OF ACTION

The day before
Main course: marinate venison

Earlier in the morning
Have equipment ready and prepare ingredients
Starter: sweat and dry mushrooms
Main course: cut venison into strips and chill; make forcemeat balls and chill; start cabbage
Dessert: make custard and spread jam

About 1 hour before the meal
Main course: cook cabbage

About 30 minutes before
Main course: bake forcemeat balls; heat water for pasta

About 15 minutes before
Main course: stir-fry and flame venison; reduce sauce and keep warm; cook pasta
Starter: sauté mushrooms

After the starter
Dessert: whisk egg whites and bake meringue
Main course: finish sauce and combine with venison

MUSHROOM FRICASSÉE

550g/1 ¼ lb mixed mushrooms, to include oyster, shiitake, brown cap and some wild mushrooms if possible
2 garlic cloves
2 tbsp oil
few coriander seeds, crushed
55g/2oz butter
1 tsp wine vinegar
2-3 sprigs of fresh coriander
sea salt and freshly ground black pepper
salad leaves, to serve
crusty white bread, to serve

Wipe the mushrooms with a clean damp tea towel or moist pads of paper towel. Pat them dry and slice or shred into attractive chunky pieces, halving or quartering the larger mushrooms.

Cut 1 of the garlic cloves in half and rub a sauté pan with the cut sides. Pour the oil into the pan and set it over a moderate heat until hot.

Add the mushrooms and sauté for about 5 minutes, stirring occasionally. Season very lightly with salt and pepper, cover and sauté for another 2-3 minutes. Tip the mushrooms from the pan into a large plate lined with a double layer of paper towels. Cover with more paper towel and leave until about 15 minutes before serving.

Then lightly wipe the sauté pan with paper towels and melt half the butter in it. Crush the remaining garlic and add this to the pan with the coriander seeds and the drained mushrooms. Season lightly and sauté for 5 minutes over a fairly high heat, stirring occasionally.

Meanwhile, line a serving dish with salad leaves.

Turn up the heat under the mushrooms, add the vinegar and snip in a few leaves of fresh coriander (don't overdo it). Then stir in the rest of the butter.

Tip the contents of the pan into the prepared dish, season again and serve immediately with crusty bread to mop up the juices.

VENISON STROGANOFF WITH FORCEMEAT BALLS

450g/1lb venison fillet
½ tbsp paprika
12 black peppercorns, crushed
1 tbsp oil
15g/½oz butter
2-3 tbsp brandy
1 tbsp redcurrant jelly
100ml/3 ½fl oz sour or single cream, plus
  extra for dribbling
sea salt and freshly ground black pepper

FOR THE MARINADE:
250ml/8fl oz red wine
1 tbsp oil
1 tsp juniper berries, crushed
1 tsp black peppercorns
2 bay leaves
3 sprigs each of parsley and thyme
½ Spanish onion, chopped

FOR THE FORCEMEAT BALLS
(MAKES ABOUT 18):
225g/8oz good sausage meat
2 heaped tbsp fresh breadcrumbs
few sprigs each of parsley, thyme and
  oregano, finely snipped
½ tsp dried sage
1 large or 2 small egg(s)
oil, for greasing
flour, for coating

The night before or early in the morning, cut the venison fillet in half and put in a bowl. Combine the ingredients for the marinade and pour it over the meat. Cover and chill, turning the pieces over once or twice.

An hour or two before the meal, drain the venison, reserving the marinade. Pat the meat thoroughly dry with paper towels or better still a clean old tea cloth (it will end up an indelible purple). Carefully cut the meat into slices about 6mm/¼in thick. Then cut these slices into strips, about 2.5cm/1in wide and 5-7.5cm/2-3in long. Pat the meat dry again, then sprinkle with paprika and press in the crushed peppercorns. Chill.

Make the forcemeat balls: in a bowl, combine all the ingredients. Season the mixture lightly with salt and liberally with pepper. Chill for at least 20 minutes.

About 1 hour before the meal, preheat the oven to 190C/375F/gas5 and grease a roasting pan with oil.

Form the chilled seasoned sausage meat into balls about the size of a large cherry tomato. Coat these in flour and arrange them in the prepared pan, leaving a little space between them. Bake for about 30 minutes, until cooked through and golden, turning them over after 15-20 minutes. Keep them warm in the switched-off oven until ready to serve.

Now cook the venison: in a wok combine the oil and butter over a high heat. Tip in the meat and stir-fry the strips for 3-4 minutes, still keeping the heat high.

Sprinkle with brandy, take the wok off the heat and carefully flame the brandy, using a long match or lighted taper. Tip the flamed venison out on a warmed plate.

Strain the reserved marinade into the wok and bring to the boil. Then cook over a moderately high heat for 8-10

minutes, letting the liquid reduce a little. Add the jelly and the cream and bring back to a simmer. Return the meat to the wok and stir for a minute or two, until heated through. Season lightly to taste.

Serve the venison with the forcemeat balls and a dribbling of cream on a bed of noodles.

RED CABBAGE HASH

450g/1lb red cabbage, shredded
2 tsp red wine vinegar
1 ½ tbsp oil
1 Spanish onion, thinly sliced
30g/1oz butter, plus extra for serving
small pinch of paprika
small pinch of ground nutmeg
small pinch of ground cinnamon
small pinch of ground allspice
2 tsp sugar
sea salt and freshly ground black pepper

Put the cabbage in a large sauté pan, cover with cold water and add a drop or two of the vinegar. Bring to the boil and then simmer for 1 minute. Drain the cabbage and reserve. Rinse and dry the sauté pan.

Heat the oil in the pan. When it is hot, add the onion. Season lightly and sauté over a low heat for a few minutes, until the onion is softened.

Now add the butter and spices and stir for a minute. Tip in the cabbage, sprinkle with the sugar and stir for a couple of minutes. Cover and cook gently for a good 50 minutes, stirring several times, until the cabbage is tender.

Sprinkle with the remaining vinegar and adjust the seasoning, if necessary. Stir in a little extra knob of butter and serve hot.

BUTTERED CARAWAY NOODLES

350g/12oz dried pappardelle or tagliatelle
1 tsp olive oil
½-1 tsp caraway seeds
few sprigs of winter savory, finely snipped,
   or ½-1 tsp dried
15-30g/½-1oz butter
sea salt and freshly ground black pepper

Bring a large pan of water to the boil with 1 teaspoon of salt and the oil. Cook the pasta at a good rolling boil until just tender but still firm.

Drain it well and return it to the pan. Stir in the caraway seeds, savory and butter. Season to taste.

Tip the contents of the pan out on a warmed serving dish and spoon the venison on top.

QUEEN OF PUDDINGS

115g/4oz fresh white bread or brioche
   crumbs
finely grated zest of ½ unwaxed lemon
finely grated zest of ½ unwaxed orange
2 tbsp vanilla sugar
575ml/1pt full-fat milk
75g/2½oz soft unsalted butter, plus extra
   for greasing
4 large eggs, separated
4-5 tbsp raspberry jam
100g/3½oz caster sugar
Chocolate Sauce (see page 49) or thick
   cream, to serve (optional)

Left *A strong combination for a chilly autumn Sunday: Venison Stroganoff with Forcemeat Balls, Buttered Caraway Noodles and Red Cabbage Hash.*

In a large bowl, combine the breadcrumbs with the grated citrus zest and the vanilla sugar.

In a small pan, bring the milk almost to the boil. Then take it off the heat, stir in the butter and pour the mixture over the flavoured breadcrumbs. Stir well, then cover and leave to soak until cool.

Preheat the oven to 180C/350F/gas4 and generously grease a gratin dish with butter.

Using a large wooden spoon, gradually beat the egg yolks into the milk mixture. Pour this custard into the prepared dish and bake for 30-40 minutes, until firm. Remove from the oven and leave to cool for at least 15 minutes. Reduce the oven temperature to 160C/325F/gas3.

In a small pan, heat the jam until just warm. Using a spatula, spread it over the cooled custard and set aside.

In a large bowl, whisk the egg whites until stiff. Spoon in half the sugar and continue whisking until shiny. Using a large metal spoon, fold in the rest of the sugar. Spoon this meringue on top of the layer of jam on the custard.

Return the pudding to the cooler oven for 30 minutes, until the meringue is golden and just crisp. Serve hot, with Chocolate Sauce or cream if wished.

PORTUGUESE PREPARATION

an unfussy cook-ahead meal

MENU

FOR 6-8

Sweet Pepper Salad
Tuna Escabèche

* * *

Pork Pot Roast with Onions
Mashed Potatoes with Bay
Stir-fried Spring Greens

* * *

Orange Tart

Y memories of Portugal are all happy ones . . . the early morning market at Oporto with its rows and rows of bright produce tended by the friendliest stallholders I have ever come across, all willing to let you taste a bite of salty cheese, an almond or a sliver of the smoked cured ham called *presunto* . . . sipping dry white port at the end of the day on a terrace overlooking the magnificent width of the Douro . . . while *en route* somewhere in the Alentejo sneaking into the kitchen of an old farmhouse (I pretended to have lost my way coming back from the ladies' room) . . . Evora with its square that is just like a set waiting for performers to start singing and dancing . . . While looking forward to my next trip, I have expanded my repertoire to include several dishes inspired by the unfussy food of Portugal.

The pork pot roast I first tasted not in Portugal, but in the middle of the Loire valley. It had been cooked by Rosa, a Portuguese friend living in my home village in the Loire. It was the Sunday between Christmas and the New Year. Rosa and her family had killed a pig and she prepared the pot roast as a gift for us. We found it succulently tender and absolutely delicious. If the loin of pork you use is not quite as young and sweet as Rosa's, double the seasoning quantities and cook for a little longer. This pot roast is one of those dishes which tastes even better reheated than first time round. In fact, most of this meal can be cooked the day before.

VEGETARIAN OPTION: I suggest an extra dish of chopped ripe avocado, dressed with a little lime or lemon juice and olive oil. This makes a great partner for the salad of sweet peppers. Also have plenty of good close-textured bread on the table. Portuguese cheeses are hard to find, but finely sliced Spanish Manchego makes a nice substitute.

TO DRINK: as an apéritif, serve Taylor's Chip Dry white port in tall glasses with ice cubes and plenty of tonic, preferably accompanied by olives and salted almonds. With the main course, try a mature Dão or Barraida red wine.

PLAN OF ACTION

The day before
Starters: make pepper salad and escabèche
Main course: pot roast pork; shred and chill greens
Dessert: bake tart

Earlier in the day
Have equipment and remaining ingredients ready
Main course: cook and mash potatoes, then cover

Shortly before eating
Starters: remove from refrigerator
Main course: reheat pork and potatoes

After the starter
Main course: stir-fry greens

TUNA ESCABÈCHE

450g/1lb fresh boneless tuna steak, about
1cm/½in thick
150ml/¼pt olive oil
1 Spanish onion, thinly sliced
2 garlic cloves, cut into slivers
1 bay leaf, cut into slivers or crumbled if
dried
¼ tsp chilli sauce
few sprigs of parsley
2-3 sprigs of thyme
½ unwaxed lemon, thinly sliced
5 tbsp wine vinegar
freshly ground black pepper

Cut the tuna into squares about 4cm/
1½in across.

Heat a tablespoon of oil in a frying
pan. Sauté the pieces of tuna, in batches,
for 2 minutes on each side over a
moderate heat. Place the sautéed fish in
an earthenware or glass dish.

Add a little more oil to the pan and
sauté the onion for 5-8 minutes, stirring
occasionally. Add the garlic, bay leaf
and chilli sauce and sauté for a few
minutes longer.

Spoon the contents of the pan over the
fish and stir to mix. Then snip over the
parsley and thyme and tuck in the slices
of lemon. Season with pepper and pour
over the rest of the oil and the vinegar.
Stir in well.

Cover and refrigerate for 24 hours.

Above *Tuna Escabèche*.

SWEET PEPPER SALAD

3 large unblemished red sweet peppers
2 large unblemished yellow sweet peppers
1 large unblemished green sweet pepper
5 tbsp strong olive oil, plus extra for
serving
1 small garlic clove, crushed
½ tsp ground coriander
2 tsp wine vinegar, plus extra for serving
sea salt and freshly ground black pepper

Preheat the oven to 200C/400F/gas6
and line a large roasting pan with a
double layer of foil to catch any juices
from the peppers.

Wash and dry the peppers. Put them side by side in the prepared pan and bake them for about 15 minutes, until the skin begins to blister. Turn the peppers over and bake for a further 10-15 minutes, until they are well charred.

Leave them until cool enough to handle, then peel off the skin, carefully collecting any cooking juices from the foil. Remove the core and all the seeds from the peppers, patting the inside with paper towels if some seeds stubbornly stick there. Cut the pepper flesh into long thin strips.

In a small bowl, combine the reserved pepper cooking juices with the olive oil, garlic, coriander and vinegar. Season lightly with salt and pepper.

Put the strips of pepper in a serving dish. Dribble over the dressing and turn the strips over. Cover with film and chill for several hours before serving (the salad will keep for 2 or 3 days in the refrigerator).

To serve, dribble over a little extra olive oil followed by a few drops of vinegar and season again lightly.

MASHED POTATOES WITH BAY

1k/2 ¼ lb waxy potatoes, peeled and boiled
150ml/ ¼ pt milk
155g/2oz soft butter, plus more if liked
3-4 bay leaves, crumbled
sea salt and freshly ground black pepper

In a small pan, heat the milk with the bay leaves until it is hot but not boiling. Push the potatoes through a vegetable mill or mash them lightly.

Melt the butter in a large saucepan.

Add the puréed potatoes and stir for a minute over a low heat.

Strain in the hot milk, a little at a time, whisking well after each addition. Season lightly with salt and more generously with pepper. Adjust the seasoning if necessary, and add a little knob of extra butter at the last minute.

If it is necessary to reheat the potato purée, cover the pan and place it over a larger pan full of boiling water. Stir occasionally and add a little more butter.

STIR-FRIED SPRING GREENS

1k/2 ¼ lb spring greens
1 large garlic clove
2 tbsp olive oil
sea salt and freshly ground black pepper
1 tbsp lemon juice, to serve (optional)

Carefully wash the greens and remove the coarse veins and stems. Dry them very thoroughly, preferably in a salad spinner. Roll up the leaves into tight little bundles and slice or snip these across to shred the leaves. Pat the shredded greens dry with paper towels, then wrap in a clean tea cloth and refrigerate for a few hours or overnight.

Shortly before serving, halve the garlic clove and rub a wok or large frying pan with the cut sides. Then sprinkle the pieces of garlic with a little salt and mash with the flat of a knife.

Heat the oil over a moderate heat, add the garlic and stir for a minute. Then tip in the chilled shredded greens and stir-fry for a few minutes.

Season and serve immediately, sprinkled with a little lemon juice.

PORK POT ROAST WITH ONIONS

1.5-1.8k/3 ½-4lb boned and rolled loin of
*   top-quality young pork, rind removed*
3-4 tbsp olive oil
3 Spanish onions, thinly sliced
2 small garlic cloves, crushed
1 tsp paprika
1 tbsp French mustard
2 bay leaves, crumbled
1 tsp rubbed sage
1 tsp dried thyme
1 tbsp tomato paste
about 150ml/ ¼ pt dry white wine
sea salt and freshly ground black pepper

Heat the oil in a large heavy-based flameproof casserole dish until extremely hot but not smoking. Brown the meat on all sides in the oil. Remove the meat from the pot and set aside.

Reduce the heat under the casserole to low. Add the onions and sweat them for several minutes, stirring occasionally until they are soft but not coloured.

Meanwhile combine the remaining ingredients except the wine. Season with a little salt and pepper and coat the browned pork with the mixture, patting it well in.

Return the pork to the pot, cover and cook for 5-10 minutes over a low heat. Then turn over and continue to cook over the low heat.

After about 10 minutes, add the wine. Put the lid back on and cook very gently for a good 2 hours, until the pork is done (the exact timing will depend on the age and quality of the meat you use). Keep the pot very tightly covered and the heat low. Turn the meat over a few times during the cooking and keep it moist with more wine, if necessary.

ORANGE TART

FOR THE SWEET SHORTCRUST PASTRY:
225g/8oz plain flour
pinch of salt
140g/5oz unsalted butter
1 egg
45g/1 ½oz caster sugar

FOR THE FILLING:
2 eggs
100g/3 ½oz caster sugar
grated zest and juice of 1 unwaxed orange
2 tsp lemon juice
2 tsp Cointreau or other orange-flavoured liqueur
85g/3oz melted unsalted butter, plus more for greasing
100g/3 ½oz ground almonds

FOR THE TOPPING:
75g/2 ½oz caster sugar
3-4 unwaxed thin-skinned oranges, thinly sliced and pips removed
1 tbsp orange marmalade
1 tsp Cointreau or other orange-flavoured liqueur
icing sugar, to dust (optional)

First make the pastry: using the metal blade of a food processor, whizz together the flour, salt and butter.

In a small bowl, combine the egg with 1 tablespoon of cold water, then stir in the sugar. Add this to the flour mixture in the food processor and whizz again in short bursts until the dough comes together into a rough ball. Wrap in cling film and chill for at least 30 minutes.

Preheat the oven to 190C/375F/gas5 and grease a large loose-bottomed tart pan with butter.

Orange Tart with a rich filling of oranges, eggs and almonds – three favourite Portuguese dessert ingredients.

Roll out the chilled pastry and use it to line the tin, pressing it into the corners gently with the hands without stretching it. Then prick the pastry all over with a fork and chill again for 10 minutes.

Line the chilled pastry case with greaseproof paper or greased foil. Fill with dried beans and bake for 15-20 minutes, until the pastry is set and the edges are brown. Turn down the oven setting to 180C/350F/gas4 and remove the beans and paper.

Make the filling: whisk the eggs and sugar until thick and creamy. Stir in the orange zest and juice, the lemon juice and the liqueur. Add the melted butter and the ground almonds and stir in thoroughly.

Pour the mixture into the baked pastry case and return to the cooler oven for about 20-25 minutes, until the orange filling is set and golden. Remove from the oven and leave to cool slightly.

Now prepare the topping: in a large pan, combine the sugar with 150ml/¼ pt water. Bring to a moderate boil, put the orange slices into the syrup and simmer gently for 3 minutes. Remove the orange slices with a slotted spoon, allowing the syrup juices to drain back into the pan, and arrange them in overlapping circles on top of the tart.

Preheat the grill to high.

Turn up the heat under the syrup pan and boil it until reduced by about half. Stir in the marmalade and liqueur and continue stirring for a minute. Liberally brush this glaze over the orange slices.

Grill the tart until the topping is very lightly caramelized, turning the tart so that it bubbles evenly and making sure the pastry edge doesn't burn. Leave to get cold.

If you like, dust the tart lightly with icing sugar just before serving. This tart can be made a day ahead and will keep for 2-3 days in a cool place in an airtight container.

DÉJEUNER SUR L'HERBE

*a traditional lunch in a
French garden*

MENU

FOR 8

*Bœuf à la Mode en Gelée
Pommes Diable
Basil Courgettes*

* * *

Colombier

88

Bœuf à la Mode en Gelée is one of the great French summer dishes . . . a classic offering at family parties, whether the occasion is a birthday, a christening, a first communion or simply a reunion. Some families will eat it in cool formal dining rooms filled with shining heavy furniture . . . everyone on best behaviour, children itching to get out. Others will be more relaxed . . . table and chairs out in the garden under the trees, everyone a little pink in the face, children still desperate to go and play. Having been brought up in the indoor tradition, I much prefer the garden alternative, even if there is a slight risk that the rich savoury beef jelly will melt on your plate rather than in your mouth.

To accompany the beef I serve Pommes Diable. Nothing complicated – the said potatoes being new potatoes cooked in an unglazed clay pot called a *diable*. The butter and cream are optional extras, since the blackened old *diable* gives them a good moist earthy taste.

I don't usually approve of Franglais recipe titles, but this is a French menu and I am allowing myself a few exceptions. I hope you will agree with me that Colombier, the French word for 'dovecot', is a more appealing name for the French-inspired dessert than strawberry macaroon.

This festive meal is easy on the Cook at the last minute, since the two *pièces de résistance* – both savoury and sweet – may be made, chilled and out of the way well in advance. The Bœuf à la Mode en Gelée is, in fact, one of those dishes best made a day ahead.

There is no 'official' starter but – as some guests are bound to be late – I suggest serving Crostini, Bresaola and Prosciutto Rolls, Flavoured Olives and Spiced Nuts (see pages 16-17) with the apéritifs.

TO DRINK: if I am truly celebrating, the apéritif has to be pink champagne. My ruinous absolute favourite is Billecart-Salmon Rosé. I would prefer to stay with a still dry rosé for the rest of the meal, but others might prefer a chilled Saint-Nicolas-de-Bourgueil or very young Beaujolais.

PLAN OF ACTION

The day before
Main course: make Bœuf à la Mode en Gelée
Dessert: make macaroon

Earlier in the morning
Dessert: prepare and chill filling
Have all the equipment ready and prepare remaining ingredients

About 1 hour before the meal
Main course: start potatoes and blanch courgettes

Few minutes before eating
Main course: finish cooking vegetables
Dessert: assemble and chill

BŒUF À LA MODE EN GELÉE

1 calf's foot, split in half
200g/7oz thick-cut rindless slices of smoked streaky bacon, chopped
1.8k/4lb rolled topside of beef, larded and barded
1 beef marrow bone, chopped
3 garlic cloves, chopped
1 Spanish onion
6 whole cloves
1 large carrot, cut in half
1 celery stalk, chopped
several sprigs each of parsley and thyme
3 bay leaves
bottle of dry white wine
sea salt and freshly ground black pepper

TO SERVE:
1.1 litre/2pt light vegetable or beef stock
18 baby onions, trimmed and peeled
350g/12oz young carrots, trimmed and sliced on the slant
250g/8 ½oz broad beans
250g/8 ½oz small French beans, topped and tailed
few leaves of chervil or flat-leaf parsley

Preheat the oven to 160C/325F/gas3.
Scrub and rinse the calf's foot and blanch it for 3 minutes in boiling water.
Heat a large heavy flameproof casserole which has a tight-fitting lid over a moderate heat. Sauté the chopped bacon in the dry pan until the fat runs. Reduce the heat a little, add the beef and patiently allow it to brown lightly but evenly on all sides in the fat.
Add the calf's foot, the chopped marrow bone, the garlic, onion studded with the cloves, the carrot, celery, parsley, thyme and bay leaves. Season and pour in the white wine. Allow the wine to come to a simmer.
Turn the beef over, fit a layer of foil under the lid of the casserole to provide a seal and cook in the oven for about 4

hours. Every hour or so, skim off any fat and turn the meat over.

Remove from the oven and leave to rest for a full 15 minutes, then transfer the beef to a dish and leave it to get cold. Strain the liquid through a fine sieve, preferably lined with muslin, into a saucepan. Reserve the calf's foot (which looks messy but tastes wonderful) for eating separately.

Prepare the vegetables for serving. Bring the stock to a simmer, season with salt if necessary, add the onions and bring the stock back to a simmer. Add the carrots, then later the broad beans and later still the French beans and cook until just tender. Drain well, refresh under cold water, drain again and pat dry with a clean tea-towel or paper towels.

Cover the beef with foil and chill it for 1 hour. Then remove the strings and pare off the outer fat. Cut the meat into thin slices, arranging them on a serving dish so that they overlap neatly. Surround the slices of beef with the onions, carrots, and beans.

Check the cooking liquid – it should be well jellied by now. Heat gently until just syrupy. If the liquid was not properly jellied, boil to reduce a little and then leave to cool and get syrupy.

Distribute the syrupy liquid over the beef and vegetables. Dot with chervil or parsley leaves and season generously with freshly ground black pepper. Cover the dish carefully with foil or film and chill until ready to serve.

Above right *Bœuf à la Mode en Gelée, served* al fresco *in the garden with a glass of chilled Tavel rosé.*

BASIL COURGETTES

900g/2lb ripe unblemished courgettes
½ garlic clove
2 tbsp olive oil
1 tsp lemon juice
15g/½oz butter
several leaves of fresh basil
sea salt and freshly ground black pepper

Trim the courgettes and cut them in half lengthwise if they are on the large side. Blanch them for 2-3 minutes in lightly salted boiling water. Drain and pat dry with paper towels. Cut the blanched courgettes into thinnish slices (about 3mm/¹⁄₁₆in thick).

Rub a sauté pan with the cut side of the garlic. Add the oil to the pan and place over a moderate heat. Tip in the courgettes, season and sauté for a few minutes, stirring occasionally.

Sprinkle in the lemon juice, cover and reduce the heat. Cook for about 3 minutes. Then turn up the heat, add the butter and stir for 1 minute.

Roll up the basil leaves and snip them over the courgettes. Adjust the seasoning and serve hot or warm.

90

POMMES DIABLE

1k/2 ¼lb new potatoes, scrubbed and well
  dried
45g/1 ½oz butter
3 tbsp cream
sprig of parsley
sea salt and freshly ground black pepper

Cook the potatoes in a *diable* on the stove
over a low heat or in the oven preheated
to 160C/325F/gas3 for about 45-50
minutes until tender. Alternatively,
steam them (see Herbed Potatoes on
page 41). Dry the pan.

　Melt the butter in the pan (or in a
clean pan if using a *diable*) over a low
heat, tip in the potatoes and spoon in the
cream. Toss lightly, snip over a little
parsley and serve hot.

COLOMBIER

1k/2 ¼lb small ripe strawberries,
  including some fraises des bois if possible
1 tbsp raspberry vinegar
575ml/1pt thick cream
2-3 tbsp kirsch
icing sugar to taste

FOR THE MACAROON:
150g/5 ½oz ground almonds
100g/3 ½oz caster sugar
100g/3 ½oz icing sugar
1 tsp juice and finely grated zest from ½
  unwaxed orange
whites of 6 eggs
butter for greasing

First prepare the macaroon: preheat the
oven to 180C/350F/gas4. Line a
baking sheet with greaseproof paper and
lightly grease this with butter.

　In a large bowl, combine the ground
almonds, caster sugar and icing sugar.

Sprinkle in the orange zest and stir.

In another large bowl, combine the egg whites with the lemon juice. Whisk until stiff but not dry. Using a large metal spoon, gently fold the whites into the almond mixture.

Spread this macaroon mixture on the prepared baking sheet in a long rectangle shape, or in 2 separate circles of the same size.

Put in the oven and reduce the temperature to 150-160C/300-325F/ gas2-3. Bake for 45-60 minutes until pale golden and cooked, occasionally checking and turning the baking sheet. Allow to cool in the oven a little before lifting the macaroon to transfer it to a wire rack. Leave to get cold.

Prepare the filling: hull the strawberries and cut the larger ones in half lengthwise. Sprinkle them with the raspberry vinegar. Whisk the cream until very firm, flavour with a little kirsch and sweeten to taste with icing sugar.

Assemble the cake: cut the macaroon rectangle into 2 identical squares, if using. Put one square or circle of macaroon on a serving dish. Set aside one-third of the strawberries, selecting as many of the smaller whole ones as possible. Then gently fold the remaining strawberries into two-thirds of the cream. Spoon this over the the macaroon square or circle. Place the second square or circle on top. Now spoon the remaining cream over the top and arrange the reserved smaller strawberries on this. Chill until ready to serve.

At the last minute, sprinkle with a little more kirsch and icing sugar.

Left *Colombier and strawberries.*

MEMORIES OF MOROCCO

a subtly spicy North-African meal

MENU

FOR 4

*Grilled Squid
with Chermoula Sauce*

* * *

*Moroccan Chicken
Steamed Marinated Vegetables*

* * *

Pistachio and Almond Filo Purses

94

MOROCCAN Chicken is one of my favourite poultry recipes. The moist nutty couscous stuffing does great things for any bird, however tough – as I remember they always seemed to be in North Africa, spending their lives scuttling in the dust under the hot sun.

A word about the sauce which I serve with the squid. In Morocco, *chermoula* tends to be used as a marinade rather than a piquant edge-of-the-plate *salsa* as here. I hope those knowledgeable about North-African food will forgive the liberty and still enjoy the seasoning.

This menu is perhaps a little more fiddly than others to prepare, but much of the work can be done in peace the day before. I always find that coaxing filo pastry into neat little parcels before it goes brittle invariably develops into a race against the clock, despite dampened tea-cloths and other protective efforts. I can only suggest having a packet or two in reserve in the refrigerator or freezer just in case someone rings you at the wrong moment.

The steamed vegetables are very much an accompaniment to the main course. If you like, have a break before dessert and serve a salad of soft and crisp lettuce leaves mixed with a few thin orange slices, dressed minimally with a little oil, salt and pepper.

The filo purses may be made the day before and chilled, then brought back to room temperature before eating.

TO DRINK: there is always Boulaouane, the dry greyish rosé that turned me into a fan of rosé at an impressionable age. What is worth brewing to serve with the dessert is mint tea, made with a little Chinese green tea, lots of cane sugar and plenty of sprigs of fresh mint all left to infuse for several minutes.

PLAN OF ACTION

The day before
Starter: prepare and chill squid; start and chill sauce
Main course: prepare and chill vegetables
Dessert: make and chill

Earlier in the morning
Main course: start chicken and couscous; take vegetables out of refrigerator
Have equipment and other ingredients ready

Shortly before eating
Dessert: take out of refrigerator
Starter: grill squid, finish sauce and assemble
Main course: leave chicken to settle in oven; moisten and heat couscous

GRILLED SQUID WITH CHERMOULA SAUCE

450g/1lb small squid
2 tbsp olive oil, plus extra for greasing
1 tbsp lemon juice
lemon wedges, to serve

FOR THE CHERMOULA SAUCE:
1 juicy garlic clove, crushed
½ tsp harissa
pinch of cumin
pinch of paprika
pinch of ground coriander
4 tbsp olive oil
2 tsp lemon juice
1 large ripe tomato, blanched, skinned, deseeded and diced
white parts of 2 large spring onions, finely chopped
several leaves of flat-leaf parsley, snipped
sea salt and freshly ground black pepper

Clean the squid. Pull the tentacles to remove all the internal organs. Cut off the tentacles just above the head, keeping them in one bunch. Discard the head and organs. Pull out and discard the translucent spine from the body pocket. Peel off and discard the pinkish external membrane. Rinse and pat dry. Slit the body into 2 flat halves and score the outside in several places with a sharp knife.

Combine the oil and lemon juice, season lightly with pepper and brush over the squid. Chill for at least 1 hour or overnight until needed.

Start the sauce: combine the garlic, harissa and spices with the oil and lemon juice and chill until needed.

Preheat the grill until hot and grease the grill pan lightly with oil. Grill the pieces of squid for about 2 minutes on each side until charred on the outside and tender inside.

Stir the diced tomato, chopped spring onion and snipped parsley into the sauce. Adjust the seasoning.

Serve the squid with the sauce and lemon wedges.

STEAMED MARINATED VEGETABLES

225g/8oz baby carrots, trimmed
350g/12oz small French green beans,
  topped and tailed
350g/12oz baby courgettes, or small ripe
  courgettes sliced on the slant
1 small Savoy cabbage, coarsely shredded
1 garlic clove, crushed
citrus pepper
2-3 sprigs of coriander
3-4 sprigs of parsley
4 tbsp olive oil
2 tsp lemon juice
sea salt and freshly ground black pepper

Bring to the boil 1.1 litre/2pt lightly salted water in a large saucepan. Add the carrots and cook them for 2 minutes. Then add the beans and cook for 1 more minute. Now throw in the courgettes and shredded cabbage and continue cooking for another 2 minutes.

Meanwhile, combine the crushed garlic, a sprinkling of citrus pepper, a sprig of coriander and 2 sprigs of parsley with 3 tablespoons of olive oil in a large salad bowl.

Drain the vegetables when all are cooked. Return them to the pan over a moderate heat and shake the pan for a few seconds until the moisture evaporates. Tip the hot vegetables into the oil mixture. Stir to coat, then adjust the seasoning if necessary. Cover, leave to get cold and then chill overnight.

Well ahead of serving, return the vegetables to room temperature.

About 20 minutes before eating, put the rest of the coriander and parsley with some lightly salted water in the bottom pan of a steamer. Bring to a simmer. Tip the vegetables into the steaming basket and discard the marinated herb sprigs. Cover and steam until hot. Then keep warm.

Just before serving, sprinkle the vegetables with the lemon juice and the remaining oil. Adjust the seasoning, if necessary, and sharpen it a little with black pepper and/or citrus pepper, if you wish.

MOROCCAN CHICKEN

1 large free-range or corn-fed chicken
300g/10 1/2oz couscous
400ml/14fl oz light chicken stock
pinch of saffron
1/2 stalk of lemon grass, split
2-3 tsp lemon juice
few sprigs of flat-leaf parsley
sea salt and freshly ground black pepper

FOR THE STUFFING:
75g/2 1/2oz unsalted butter, softened
2 tbsp runny honey
55g/2oz pine kernels
55g/2oz raisins
2 baby onions, finely chopped
1 garlic clove, crushed
1/2 tsp harissa
1/2 tsp ground cinnamon
1 tsp ground cumin
1 tsp ground ginger
1 tsp ground coriander

Rinse the chicken inside and out and dry well.

Cook the couscous according to the instructions on the packet, but using only three-quarters of the amount of liquid specified – the couscous will go on absorbing juices while the chicken is being cooked.

Make the stuffing: in a large bowl, combine half the cooked couscous with the stuffing ingredients, reserving a good knob of butter. Toss until well mixed, then season with salt and pepper.

Lightly rub the main cavity of the chicken with salt and spoon in the stuffing without packing it in too tightly. Return the rest of the stuffing to the cooked couscous. Sew up the chicken and truss it if you like.

In a large deep flameproof casserole dish, bring to a simmer the stock, together with the saffron and lemon grass. Add the chicken and return the liquid to a light boil over a moderate heat. Then cover tightly and simmer for about 20 minutes, keeping the heat fairly low. Turn the chicken over and cook for a further 20 minutes.

Towards the end of this process, preheat the oven to 220C/425F/gas7.

Transfer the chicken to a roasting pan and cook in the oven for a good 30 minutes, until golden and cooked through. Leave to settle in the switched-off oven for 10 minutes. Reserve the cooking liquid.

Meanwhile, gently heat the rest of the couscous mixture in a sauté pan. Moisten it with a few tablespoons of the chicken cooking liquid. Stir in the reserved butter and keep over a low heat until tender. Adjust the seasoning and keep warm.

Bring the rest of the cooking liquid to the boil and reduce by about a quarter.

Just before serving, adjust the seasoning of the liquid and sharpen it with a little lemon juice. Surround the chicken with couscous on a serving platter and scatter with parsley leaves. Dribble a little liquid through a fine sieve over the chicken to moisten. Strain the rest of the liquid into a warmed sauce boat.

PISTACHIO AND ALMOND FILO PURSES

8 sheets of filo pastry
115g/4oz very soft unsalted butter

FOR THE SYRUP:
200g/7oz caster sugar
1 tbsp lemon juice
1 tbsp rose water
1 tbsp orange blossom water

FOR THE FILLING:
85g/3oz shelled pistachio nuts
45g/1 ½oz ground almonds
140g/5oz cream cheese or Mascarpone
pinch of freshly ground green cardamom

Preheat the oven to 200C/400F/gas6.

Prepare the syrup: in a small heavy saucepan combine the sugar with about 175ml/6fl oz water. Bring to the boil and then simmer gently.

Meanwhile make the filling: coarsely grind half the shelled pistachio nuts. In a bowl, combine them with the ground almonds, cheese and cardamom. Roughly chop the rest of the pistachio nuts and reserve.

Now make the purses: using a saucer set over very hot water, melt the butter. Keeping the sheets of pastry not being used well covered with a damp clean tea towel to stop them drying out, cut one of the filo sheets in half.

Using a wide brush, butter one side of each half. Place one on top of the other, buttered sides up. Cut the double sheet again in half to make two identical rectangles. Now make the rectangles into a cross, placing one half over the other.

Place one-eighth of the filling in the centre of the cross, lift up the corners and bring them together around the filling to make a little purse and pinch to close. Tie with a little fine string or satin ribbon. Brush the purse with a little more butter. Make 7 more purses in the same way, working as swiftly as is possible.

Bake the purses for about 15 minutes, until golden brown and crisp. Brush any remaining butter over the top of the purses then allow them to cool.

Stir the lemon juice, rose water and orange blossom water into the syrup. Then add the reserved pistachio nuts and cook for another few minutes. Leave to cool a little, then spoon the syrup over the warm filo purses. Leave to get completely cold before serving.

Right *Crunchy sweetness and creamy filling: Pistachio and Almond Filo Purses. Savour slowly between sips of Mint Tea or black coffee.*

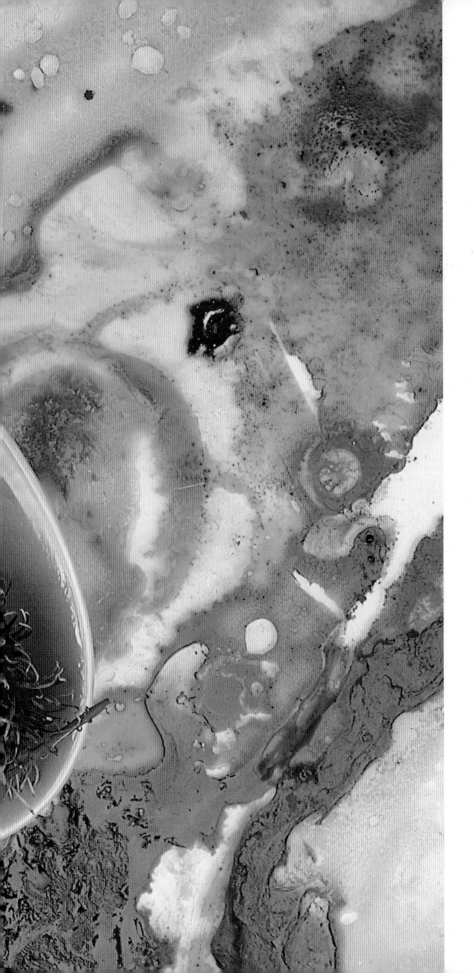

LOOKING
TO THE EAST

an almost Oriental meal

MENU

FOR 6

Orange and Ginger Duck
Fragrant Rice
Stir-fried Pak-choi with
Water Chestnuts
Mixed Salad with a Sweet
Tarragon Dressing

* * *

Fruits Rafraîchis Exotiques

100

CRISPY offering that I hope will please duck lovers of both the French and Chinese persuasion, my Orange and Ginger Duck is inspired both by *canard à l'orange* and by Peking duck – probably more by the latter. If you prefer not to shred your duck, allow one small breast per person – it will 'present' better than a large breast for 2 – reducing the first roasting time by 10 minutes and the last one by about 5.

VEGETARIAN OPTION: I like to serve Mushroom Fricassée (page 74), also in lettuce boats. Throw a good handful of peanuts, cashew nuts or pine nuts into the pak-choi with the water chestnuts.

SHOPPING: pak-choi is, I believe, part of the cabbage family – Chinese branch. It seems to be regularly on sale in my local supermarket as well as in stores specializing in 'Far-Eastern' products. If you cannot find any, use pe-tsai or Chinese cabbage, or a mix of spinach and spring greens, or broccoli florets.

TO DRINK: keep in the spirit of the duck by serving an Alsace Riesling with plenty of green or Jasmine tea.

PLAN OF ACTION

Earlier in the morning
Dessert: make syrup, cool and assemble, then chill
Prepare equipment and ingredients

About 1 3/4 hours before the meal
Main course: start preparing duck; make salad dressing

About 30 minutes before
Main course: start cooking rice

Shortly before eating
Main course: cook pak-choi; shred duck; finish sauce; assemble salad

ORANGE AND GINGER DUCK

3 large duck breasts, each weighing about 300g/10 1/2 oz
2-3 tbsp runny honey
sea salt and freshly ground black pepper

FOR THE SAUCE:
250ml/8fl oz chicken stock
200ml/7fl oz orange juice
1 tbsp grated zest from an unwaxed orange
3.5cm/1 1/2in piece of peeled fresh root ginger, finely chopped
1 large fresh garlic clove, finely chopped
1/2 tbsp light soy sauce
2 tbsp dry sherry or 1 tbsp brandy
pinch of chilli powder
15g/1/2oz chilled butter, diced

TO SERVE:
6-9 large unblemished concave leaves from a crisp fresh round lettuce such as butterhead, buttercrunch or four seasons
fine strips of unwaxed orange zest, blanched (optional)

Well ahead of cooking, using a sharp knife, deeply score the skin of the duck breasts several times. Using a brush, coat the duck breasts all over with honey. Season generously with salt and pepper, pressing the seasoning in well with a palette knife. Leave for at least 30 minutes to marinate.

Preheat the oven to 230C/450F/gas8.

Put the stock in a heavy-based saucepan. In a bowl, combine the orange juice with the remaining sauce ingredients, except the butter.

Half fill a roasting pan with boiling water and place the duck breasts, skin side up, on a rack over it. Roast for 30 minutes, basting the duck 2 or 3 times with a few spoonfuls of the orange juice mixture. If the duck blackens and smokes alarmingly, turn the heat down to 220C/425F/gas7.

Turn the duck breasts over, baste with more orange juice mixture and continue roasting, skin side down, for 10 minutes.

Reduce the oven setting to 160C/325F/gas3, turn the duck over once more and continue roasting for 20-30 minutes, basting occasionally with the orange juice mixture.

While the duck is cooking, bring the chicken stock to the boil. Reduce the heat and simmer until it is reduced by half. Keep hot. When the duck is nearly cooked, add the orange juice mixture to the reduced stock. Bring to the boil, then reduce the heat and simmer, stirring occasionally, until reduced a little. Keep hot.

Leave the duck to settle in the warm oven for 10 minutes or so and warm a large serving platter and a sauce boat.

Using a small sharp knife, cut off the duck skin. Cut the skin into thin strips and keep warm. Now cut the flesh into strips. Pile the duck flesh into the lettuce 'cups', scatter a few strips of skin on top and moisten with a little sauce. If you like, sprinkle with a few fine strips of blanched orange zest. Arrange these on the platter around the Fragrant Rice with the Stir-fried Pak-choi with Water Chestnuts.

To finish the sauce, whisk the diced chilled butter into it. Adjust the seasoning and strain the sauce into the warmed sauce boat.

Right *Serve them together: Orange and Ginger Duck, Fragrant Rice and Stir-fried Pak-choi with Water Chestnuts.*

102

FRAGRANT RICE

*350g/12oz good long-grain rice such as
    Basmati, Jasmine or Patna*
stalk of fresh lemon grass
4 small spring onions
3 tbsp oil
*1 small red chilli pepper, deseeded
    (optional)*
sea salt and freshly ground black pepper

Rinse the rice well under cold running
water until the water runs clear.

Cut off the outer leaves of the lemon
grass and cut them across into 2
segments each. Reserve the tender core
stem. Chop the white parts of the spring
onions and reserve the best of the green
parts.

Heat half the oil in a large heavy-
based saucepan. Sauté the pieces of
spring onion white in it for 1 minute,
then scatter in the rice and stir for 1
minute.

Add plenty of boiling salted water and
the cut lemon grass outer leaves and
cook until tender but still a little firm.
Drain the rice and discard the boiled
lemon grass.

Return the pan to the heat and add the
rest of the oil. Then tip in the drained
rice and stir for 1 minute.

Take off the heat, snip in very fine
pieces of lemon grass core and the
reserved pieces of spring onion. If you
like, also snip in a few very fine pieces
of red chilli pepper. Season lightly and
cover the pan.

Leave to stand for a few minutes,
then stir and serve at once.

Right *Waiting to be used: exotic
ingredients for a Sunday lunch with more
than a hint of the Orient.*

STIR-FRIED PAK-CHOI WITH WATER CHESTNUTS

675g/1 ½lb pak-choi
225g/8oz canned water chestnuts, drained,
  rinsed and drained again
1-1 ½ tbsp oil
salt and freshly ground black pepper
1 ½ tbsp light soya sauce
3 tbsp oyster sauce

Separate the leaves of the pak-choi and cut off the tough base of the stems. Wash and cut into 7.5cm/3in pieces no wider than 4cm/½in. Cut the water chestnuts into very thin slices.

Heat the oil in a wok until very hot. Tip in the pak-choi and stir-fry over a high heat for 2 minutes.

Add 2 or 3 tablespoons of water, season very lightly with salt and more generously with pepper. Stir in the soya sauce and the oyster sauce, then add the water chestnuts and stir until hot.

Serve at once.

MIXED SALAD WITH A SWEET TARRAGON DRESSING

1 small cucumber, peeled, halved
  lengthwise, deseeded and very thinly
  sliced
1 cos lettuce, leaves separated and torn into
  manageable pieces
crisp round lettuce leaves
few radicchio leaves, shredded
several flat-leaf parsley leaves
several tarragon leaves
1 tbsp oil

FOR THE DRESSING:
2 tbsp white wine vinegar
1 scant tsp sugar
2 tsp sea salt
freshly ground black pepper
several tarragon leaves, finely snipped

First make the dressing by whisking together the ingredients with one tablespoon of water.

In a salad bowl, combine the cucumber slices with the various leaves and herbs. Sprinkle with the oil and toss together.

Dribble in the dressing, toss well again and serve.

Above right *Fruits Rafraîchis Exotiques*
make a refreshing dessert – sweet but with
a sharpish bite.

FRUITS RAFRAÎCHIS EXOTIQUES

12-18 fresh lychees, peeled and halved
12 fresh cape gooseberries, papery skin
  removed
3-4 kumquats, thinly sliced
1 star fruit, thinly sliced
1large wedge of water melon, scooped into
  balls
few slices of fresh pineapple, chopped
lime juice, to serve

FOR THE SYRUP:
1 Jasmine tea or Earl Grey tea bag
100g/3 ½oz sugar

First make the syrup. Infuse the tea bag in 250ml/8fl oz boiling water for a few minutes. Remove the tea bag and then discard.

In a small heavy-based saucepan, combine the infusion with the sugar and bring to the boil. Leave to bubble gently until reduced by about half. Set aside until cold.

In a bowl, combine the pieces of fruit. Sprinkle with the cold sugar syrup, toss gently and chill until needed.

Sprinkle with a little lime juice just before serving.

VEGETARIAN MUNIFICENCE

a splendidly varied meat-free meal

MENU

FOR 8-10

The Munificent Spread

* * *

*Aubergine Parmigiana
Broccoli and Cauliflower Florets*

* * *

Walnut Cake with Poached Plums

I LOVE starters and appetizers and my Munificent Spread is in the spirit of the *antipasto misto* that generously bids you welcome to an Italian meal. My friend – and respected fellow food-writer – Anna del Conte describes the unrivalled *hors d'œuvre* of her country as 'a joy to the eye and a promise of the delights to come'. I couldn't agree more.

In fact, this meal is built around a spectacularly generous assortment of *antipasto*. If you want to have this on the table for your guests to admire when they arrive, you will need to make plenty of room at the centre. Get out your most colourful and prettiest serving dishes – the greater the variety the better. Serve each item on separate plates or arrange selections on several large platters.

To get the full benefit of their flavours, serve the *antipasto* at room temperature rather than chilled. The main course, on the other hand, will really taste better served piping hot.

TO DRINK: a good Pinot Grigio from Friuli to accompany the starter; then, for those who prefer to move on to red, a Barolo or Chianti.

PLAN OF ACTION

The day before
Starter: prepare and chill Sweet Pepper Salad, Fennel and Orange Salad and Grilled Artichoke Hearts and Courgette Slices; hard-boil quails' eggs
Dessert: make cake and poach plums

Earlier in the morning
Main course: make sauce, prepare dish and start baking; keep warm until ready for topping with Parmesan and browning
Prepare equipment and ingredients

About 1 hour before the meal
Starter: finish preparing

Shortly before eating
Main course: brown gratin and cook broccoli and cauliflower florets

THE MUNIFICENT SPREAD

Sweet Pepper Salad (see page 82)
about 100g/3 ¹/₂oz black and green olives, flavoured if liked (see page 17)
85g/3oz rocket leaves
sea salt and freshly ground black pepper

Above right *First, appeal to the eye: an assortment of antipasto that will whet everybody's appetite.*

FOR THE FENNEL AND ORANGE SALAD:
3 small fennel bulbs, trimmed and cut in half lengthwise
about 2 tbsp good-quality olive oil
1 tbsp orange juice
few sprigs of tarragon, snipped

FOR THE GRILLED ARTICHOKE HEARTS AND COURGETTE SLICES:
4 small ripe firm courgettes
225g/8oz canned or bottled artichoke hearts, drained well
4-5 tbsp Vinaigrette Gourmande (see Asperges Gourmandes on page 55) or good-quality olive oil

FOR THE HOT QUAILS' EGGS:
12 hard-boiled quails' eggs, shelled and halved lengthwise (or 4 hard-boiled standard eggs)
few drops of Tabasco
few drops of Worcestershire sauce
few drops of brown sauce or mushroom ketchup
few drops of lemon juice
about 1 tsp hot mustard
cayenne pepper
soft lettuce leaves, to serve (optional)

FOR THE MOZZARELLA AND TOMATO SALAD:
225g/8oz Mozzarella cheese, cut into thin strips
3 large ripe tomatoes, thinly sliced and most of the seeds removed
3-4 tbsp good-quality olive oil
1 tbsp lemon juice
1 tbsp snipped chives

FOR THE RED PEARS WITH PARMESAN:
3 ripe red Williams pears, unpeeled and thinly sliced
75g/2 ¹/₂oz fresh Parmesan cheese, shaved into thin slivers

To make the Mozzarella and Tomato Salad: arrange alternating strips of Mozzarella and slices of tomato overlapping on a serving plate. Season lightly with salt and more generously with pepper. Then dribble over a little olive oil and a few drops of lemon juice. Scatter with snipped chives.

To make the Red Pears with Parmesan: arrange the slices of pear and slivers of Parmesan in the same way as the tomatoes and Mozzarella and season with black pepper.

BROCCOLI AND CAULIFLOWER FLORETS

400g/14oz unblemished cauliflower, separated into florets
400g/14oz unblemished broccoli, separated into florets
55g/2oz unsalted butter
1 tsp lemon juice
paprika
sea salt and freshly ground black pepper

Bring a large pan of salted water to the boil. Add the cauliflower and return the pan to the boil as quickly as possible. Then add the broccoli and cook until it is done to taste but not disintegrating. Drain well.

Return the pan to a low heat and melt the butter in it. Tip the butter into a small cup, add the lemon juice and a little pepper and paprika.

Return the drained cauliflower and broccoli florets to the pan. Turn off the heat and pour in the butter. Toss the vegetables lightly to coat them well and serve hot.

If you do not intend to serve the vegetables immediately, slightly undercook them and reheat later.

To make the Fennel and Orange Salad: blanch the prepared fennel bulbs in salted boiling water for 4-5 minutes.

Meanwhile, preheat the grill to high. Drain the fennel well and squeeze dry between sheets of paper towels. Dribble a little oil over the fennel and grill for 3-5 minutes.

Sprinkle the cooked fennel with orange juice, season with salt and black pepper and scatter over a little snipped tarragon. Leave to get cold.

To make the Grilled Artichoke Hearts and Courgette Slices: first preheat the grill to high. Cut the courgettes in half lengthwise, then, using a vegetable peeler, thinly slice them also lengthwise. Blanch the courgette slices for 1 minute in lightly salted water, then drain thoroughly and pop them under the hot grill for 1-2 minutes. If you prefer, use a griddle to achieve the same barely charred effect. Dribble the grilled courgettes and artichoke hearts with a little of the vinaigrette dressing or olive oil. Leave to get cold.

To make the Hot Quails' Eggs: in a small cup or saucer, combine a few drops each of Tabasco, the other sauces and lemon juice. Stir in a tiny amount of mustard and season with a very little cayenne, salt and black pepper. Dip the base of each halved quail's egg into this mixture.

Serve on a bed of soft lettuce leaves or scattered around the antipasto platter.

If you prefer to use hard-boiled hens' eggs, carefully halve them lengthwise. Then gently lift out the yolk, spoon a touch of hot sauce into the cavity and replace the yolk.

AUBERGINE PARMIGIANA

2 even-sized large aubergines
1 large or 2 small egg(s), beaten with a
*   little milk*
about 115g/4oz dried breadcrumbs
about 150ml/¼pt olive oil
200g/7oz fresh Ricotta cheese
200g/7oz Mozzarella cheese, cut into thin
*   strips*
100g/3½oz fresh Parmesan cheese, grated
30g/1oz butter
sea salt and freshly ground black pepper
flour for coating
few leaves of basil, snipped, to garnish
*   (optional)*

FOR THE TOMATO SAUCE:
575ml/1pt good passata or 675g/1½lb
*   canned peeled tomatoes, drained*
100ml/3½fl oz red wine
2 tsp sugar
2 juicy garlic cloves, crushed
white parts of 2 spring onions, finely
*   chopped*
1 tsp dried oregano
2 tsp dried thyme

First make the sauce: combine the ingredients in a heavy-based saucepan and season lightly. Bring to a simmer and cook for 20-30 minutes, stirring occasionally, until slightly thickened and reduced.

Meanwhile preheat the oven to 180C/350F/gas4 and cut the unpeeled aubergines lengthwise into slices about 2cm/¾in thick.

Have three shallow bowls ready. In the first bowl tip some flour and season it. Pour the egg mixture into the second bowl (you may need to add more milk as you go along). Put the breadcrumbs in the third bowl. Have plenty of paper towels ready.

In a large heavy frying pan swirl enough olive oil to coat the base and sides generously and place over a moderate heat.

Dip some aubergine slices, one at a time, into the seasoned flour, then into the egg mixture and finally into the breadcrumbs so that they are lightly coated, shaking off excess each time. Sauté them in the frying pan, a few at a time, until nicely browned on both sides. Keep the heat low to moderate (take the pan off the heat briefly every so often) to make sure the aubergine does not burn. Remove the sautéed slices with a fish slice and drain well on the paper towels. Cook the rest in the same careful way, adding a little more oil to the pan between batches. Keep the heat moderate.

Arrange the sautéed aubergines side by side tightly in a large gratin dish. Cover with the Ricotta and then the Mozzarella. Bake for 30-40 minutes.

Turn up the oven setting to 220C/ 425F/gas7 and take the dish out of the oven. Sprinkle it evenly with the grated Parmesan, dot with the butter and return to the oven for a further 15-20 minutes, until golden brown.

If you like, sprinkle some snipped basil leaves over the dish just before serving piping hot. Adjust the seasoning of the sauce, if necessary, and serve separately in a warm bowl.

WALNUT CAKE WITH POACHED PLUMS

FOR THE WALNUT CAKE:
285g/10oz very fresh walnut kernels
3 eggs, separated
225g/8oz caster sugar, plus extra for
*   sautéing*
75g/2½oz self-raising flour, plus extra
*   for flouring*
1 tbsp kirsch
butter for greasing

FOR THE POACHED PLUMS:
125g/4½oz caster sugar
3 tbsp white wine
675g/1½lb mixed ripe but firm plums,
*   preferably including some greengages and*
*   mirabelles*
3 tbsp rum or kirsch
Greek-style yogurt and/or fromage frais, to
*   serve*

First make the walnut cake: preheat the oven to 180C/350F/gas4 and generously butter and flour a *moule à manqué* or deep flan pan.

Reserve 12-15 pretty walnut kernels and whizz the rest in a blender or food processor until coarsely ground.

Whisk the egg yolks with the sugar until smooth and pale. Stir in the ground walnuts, then sift in the flour and sprinkle in the kirsch. Whisk lightly until the mixture is smooth.

Whisk the egg whites until stiff. Then, using a large metal spoon, fold them lightly but thoroughly into the flour mixture.

Pour the cake mixture into the pan. Knock it a couple of times against the work surface to settle it and remove air pockets. Bake for 35-45 minutes, until the cake is cooked and springs back firmly to the touch when pressed. Leave it to cool for a while in the pan, then turn it out on a rack and leave to cool.

Meanwhile prepare the reserved nuts: lightly grease a small frying pan with butter and heat it through over a moderate heat. Scatter in the nuts and sauté them for a few minutes, shaking the pan occasionally. Sprinkle with a little sugar and sauté for another minute or so. Remove from the heat and reserve.

Now poach the plums: in a heavy-based saucepan, combine the sugar with the white wine and about 250ml/8fl oz water. Bring to a gentle boil and leave the syrup to simmer gently.

Meanwhile, using a small sharp knife, remove the stones from the plums, trying to leave them whole.

Using a spoon, lower half the plums into the simmering syrup and poach them until just cooked. Lift them out with a slotted spoon, allowing all the juices to drip back into the pan. Put the cooked plums in a serving dish and poach the rest in the syrup.

Select 2 or 3 of the most bruised or soft plums. Mash them lightly and return them to the syrup. Turn up the heat a little and cook for a further 5 minutes, until the plums are mushy and the syrup is slightly reduced.

Push the syrup and plum mixture through a fine sieve into a small cup. Stir in a tablespoon of rum or kirsch. Spoon or brush a little flavoured syrup over the cake and arrange the prepared walnut kernels over the top.

Add the rest of the rum or kirsch to the syrup in the cup and dribble this over the plums. Serve cold with the cake and some yogurt.

Left *Walnut Cake with Poached Plums. Make with top-quality walnut kernels for best flavour.*

LAID-BACK
BUFFET

*feeding a crowd without
spending a fortune*

MENU

FOR 10 OR MORE

*Vegetable Chilli
Jambon Persillé
Tabbouleh
Gratin Dauphinois
Salade Gourmande
Chocolate Cake*

112

THE dishes in this chapter are perfect for those informal occasions when your guests will come to eat well and have a jolly time rather than hang around picking decorously at some exquisite little canapés. The recipes have been tested on the most varied of people over the years in London and in the Loire and, yes, they do seem happy to come back for more helpings of the same.

A buffet of this nature should be flexible. Dishes I often include and which you might like to try as alternatives or supplements are Pissaladière (page 12), Salmon Rillettes (page 12-13), Tortilla Habershon (page 52-3), Glazed Chicken Drumsticks (page 53), the Munificent Spread (page 106-7) and Simple Trifle (page 70). In this way it may also be made entirely suitable for vegetarians.

TO DRINK: Australian Semillon Chardonnay and a fruity light red, such as Côtes du Ventoux from the Southern Rhône, with lots of mineral water, lager and soft drinks.

PLAN OF ACTION

Two days before
Make Jambon Persillé

The day before
Start chilli and chill
Make Chocolate Cake
Make and chill Tabbouleh

Earlier in the day
Make Gratin Dauphinois; prepare salad and dressing
Have all equipment and remaining ingredients ready

About 1 hour before the party
Finish chilli and keep warm

Shortly before the party
Assemble salad; put berries around chocolate cake

VEGETABLE CHILLI

SERVES 8 AS MAIN COURSE OR 16 AS SIDE DISH

2 tsp sesame oil
6 tbsp groundnut or sunflower oil
1 1/2 Spanish onions, finely chopped
6 garlic cloves, crushed
1 1/2 tbsp chilli powder or harissa
2 tsp paprika
2 tsp ground cloves
2 tsp ground cinnamon
2 tsp ground coriander
2 tsp ground cumin
2 tsp oregano
300ml/ 1/2 pt red wine
800g/ 1 3/4 lb canned chopped tomatoes
2 tbsp tomato paste
800g/ 1 3/4 lb canned kidney beans, well drained
400ml/14fl oz vegetable stock, plus more if required
2 tbsp sesame seeds
700g/ 1 1/2 lb mixed chopped vegetables, such as broccoli and cauliflower florets, mange-tout peas, baby sweetcorn, deseeded sweet pepper and courgettes
sea salt and freshly ground black pepper

TO SERVE:
finely snipped fresh coriander leaves
1 avocado, sliced and brushed with lemon juice
crusty bread
fromage frais mixed with yogurt
grated Cheddar cheese
finely chopped onion

Heat 1 teaspoon of the sesame oil with 2 tablespoons of the groundnut or sunflower oil in a heavy-based sauté pan and sauté the onion and garlic over a moderate heat until soft but not coloured.

Add the spices and herbs and stir for a couple of minutes. Add one-third of the wine and cook until it evaporates, still stirring. Add the tomatoes and their

liquid, the tomato paste, the drained beans, the rest of the wine and the stock.

Simmer gently uncovered for 45 minutes, stirring occasionally, until the mixture is a good thick consistency. Taste and adjust the spices and seasoning towards the end of cooking. Leave to get cold and chill overnight (or freeze) if cooking ahead.

In a large frying pan, heat the remaining oils. Stir in the sesame seeds, then add the prepared vegetables and sauté for 3-4 minutes, stirring all the time.

Meanwhile, if the chilli mixture has been prepared ahead and chilled or frozen, gently reheat it.

Add the vegetables to the hot chilli mixture and cook for a further 10 minutes, adding a little extra stock if the dish looks too solid. Season lightly with salt and pepper, if necessary.

Serve hot, warm or at room temperature, with snipped coriander, avocado slices, plenty of bread, bowls of grated Cheddar, chopped onion and the fromage frais mixed with yogurt.

To make meat chilli, omit the mixed vegetables and use 900g/2lb lean beef or lamb. Sauté the onions and herbs as above, then remove from the pan.

Add the rest of the oil and the sesame seeds and turn up the heat to high. Slap the meat into the pan and press it hard to seize it. Leave for 3-5 minutes, then break up the meat. Stir and press down again, still over a high heat, for 5-10 minutes. Now break up this 'cake' of meat and turn the pieces of meat over until evenly browned.

Return the onions to the pan, stir them into the meat and continue cooking as above.

Unlike vegetable chilli which is fine served *tiède* or cold, meat chilli should really be served piping hot.

Left *On the buffet table: Salade Gourmande and plenty of fresh fruit.*

JAMBON PERSILLÉ

SERVES 10

1.8k/4lb uncooked ham or gammon, or a
   mixture of both
1 veal knuckle
2 beef marrow bones, chopped
1 calf's foot, split and blanched
2 bay leaves
2 small bunches of flat-leaf parsley
several sprigs of thyme
several sprigs of tarragon
16 black peppercorns
1 bottle dry white wine
several sprigs of chervil, snipped
2 tsp dried marjoram
freshly ground black pepper

TO SERVE:
gherkins
hot mustard
watercress salad
plenty of bread

Put the ham and/or gammon in a very
large pan. Cover with cold water and
bring to the boil. Then remove from the
heat, pour out the water and start again
with fresh cold water. Once you have
repeated the procedure, rinse the pan
and meat. Drain the meat again and
return it to the pan. Cover with water
and bring back to a gentle boil over a
moderate heat and simmer gently for 30
minutes, skimming off scum as it rises.

Discard the liquid and rinse out the
pan. Leave the meat to cool a little, then
cut it into chunks, discarding any excess
fat or tough rind.

Return the meat to the pan with the
veal knuckle, marrow bones, calf's foot,
bay leaves, one of the bunches of
parsley, the thyme, half the tarragon,
the peppercorns and wine. Top with just
enough water to cover. Bring to a

Above *Jambon Persillé. Jellied ham
traditionally eaten at Easter in Burgundy,
makes a great buffet dish.*

simmer and cook gently for about 1½
hours, skimming off the greyish fat as it
comes up.

Lift out the ham pieces and leave
them to cool in a large bowl. Strain the
cooking liquid into another bowl
through a fine sieve lined with muslin
and discard the other ingredients.

Lightly flake the ham and snip the
remaining parsley and tarragon.
Combine the flaked ham with the
snipped herbs, the chervil, marjoram
and a little cooking liquid. Season
generously with black pepper.

Spoon a little cooking liquid into an
attractive loaf tin or terrine dish, add
the herbed ham flakes, then more
cooking liquid to cover. Knock hard on
a work surface to settle the contents.
Leave until cold. Then cover,
refrigerate overnight, or for up to 48
hours.

Serve straight from the dish or turned
out and sliced, accompanied by a bowl
of gherkins, hot mustard, watercress
salad and plenty of bread.

TABBOULEH

SERVES 16

450g/1lb bulghar wheat
1 small cucumber, peeled, deseeded and
   finely chopped
1 Spanish onion, finely chopped
450g/1lb tomatoes, blanched, skinned,
   deseeded and finely chopped or 400g/
   14oz canned chopped tomatoes, drained
2 tsp ground coriander
small bunch of flat-leaf parsley, finely
   snipped
several sprigs of fresh mint, finely snipped
6-8 tbsp olive oil
juice of 1 large ripe lemon
juice of ½ lime
55g/2oz pine kernels
sea salt and freshly ground black pepper

TO SERVE:
few small bunches of mint
12 black pitted olives, halved
few small spring onions, halved

Cook or soak the bulghar according to
the instructions on the packet, but using
only three-quarters of the amount of
liquid required or allowing only two-
thirds of the time specified. Drain well

and squeeze to get rid of any excess moisture – the grains will go on absorbing juices from the other ingredients.

Combine with the prepared cucumber, onion, tomatoes, coriander, parsley and mint. Sprinkle in the olive oil and lemon and lime juice. Toss until well moistened, then season lightly with salt and freshly ground black pepper. Cover and leave to stand for 2-3 hours in a cool place.

At the end of this time, toss again and adjust the seasoning, adding extra oil, lemon juice or more snipped mint leaves if necessary. Mix in the pine kernels.

Cover and keep cool for 1 hour or until needed. Sprinkle the tabbouleh with mint leaves, black olives and spring onions just before putting the dish on the buffet.

GRATIN DAUPHINOIS

SERVES 10

1k/2 ¼ lb large waxy potatoes
3 juicy garlic cloves
55g/2oz butter, plus more for greasing
350ml/12fl oz single cream
100ml/3 ½fl oz full-fat milk
yolk of 1 large egg
pinch of freshly ground nutmeg
pinch of cayenne pepper
55g/2oz strongly flavoured Gruyère cheese, grated
sea salt and freshly ground black pepper

Preheat the oven to 160C/325F/gas3. Peel and thinly slice the potatoes.

Cut one of the garlic cloves and use the cut sides to rub a large gratin dish. Crush all the garlic and reserve. Then grease the dish well with butter.

Heat the cream and milk until warm. Then take off the heat and stir in the egg yolk. Season lightly with nutmeg,

cayenne, salt and pepper. Stir in the reserved crushed garlic.

Arrange a layer of potato slices in the prepared dish. Season lightly with salt and pepper, spoon over some of the cream mixture. Repeat with the rest of the potatoes, ending up with a good layer of cream. Dot the surface with butter.

Bake for 1 hour. Take out of the oven and turn up the setting to 200C/400F/gas6. Sprinkle the gratin with the grated cheese, dot with more butter and season with pepper. Return to the oven for a further 20 minutes. Check with a skewer to make sure that the potatoes are tender. If not, turn down the heat to its original setting, bake for 10 more minutes and turn the heat back up for a final 5 minutes.

Eat warm rather than hot.

SALADE GOURMANDE

SERVES 8-10

1 cos lettuce
1 soft lettuce
1 oak leaf lettuce
bunch of watercress
few radicchio leaves
1 small mouli (daikon) or long pink radish, thinly sliced
200g/7oz canned palm hearts, drained and shredded
2 ripe avocados
1 tbsp lemon juice
55g/2oz fresh pecan or walnut kernels
several sprigs each of flat-leaf parsley and chervil, snipped
small bunch of chives, snipped

FOR THE DRESSING:
1 hard-boiled egg, grated
100ml/3 ½fl oz olive oil
1 tbsp French mustard
2 tbsp sherry vinegar
3 tbsp single cream
3 tbsp Greek-style yogurt
few drops of Tabasco
few drops of Worcestershire sauce
2-3 tsp tomato ketchup
sea salt and freshly ground black pepper

First prepare the dressing: whizz together all ingredients except the Tabasco, Worcestershire sauce, ketchup, salt and pepper. Then season and adjust the consistency with the remaining ingredients to taste – the dressing should be creamy but piquant. Chill until needed. Take out of the refrigerator 30 minutes before dressing the salad.

Wash the salad leaves and drain them well in a salad spinner, in several batches. Shred the radicchio and the larger leaves. Line a very large shallow bowl or deep serving platter with half the salad leaves. Scatter in half the mouli slices and palm hearts.

Peel, stone and slice the avocados. Brush with lemon juice and distribute half the prepared avocado over the salad. Sprinkle with a few nuts and one-third of the snipped herbs.

Spoon over half the dressing and toss gently but well, using your hands if you like. Repeat this process, using the rest of the avocados and half the remaining nuts and herbs.

Scatter the remaining nuts and herbs over the top after the final dressing and tossing.

CHOCOLATE CAKE

SERVES 8

175g/6 ½oz softened unsalted butter plus 1
    tbsp chilled for the coating and more for
    greasing
425g/15oz best-quality bitter chocolate,
    broken into small pieces
150g/5 ½oz caster sugar
3 heaped tbsp self-raising flour
5 eggs, separated
pinch of salt
grated zest of 1 small unwaxed orange
3 tbsp Cointreau or orange juice
3 tbsp thin-cut orange marmalade
3 tbsp single cream
2-3 tsp icing sugar (optional)

TO SERVE:
450g/1lb mixed soft fruit
sprigs of mint
bowl of whisked crème fraîche sweetened
    with a little icing sugar

Preheat the oven to 180C/350F/gas4
and generously butter a large loaf or
round cake pan, then line it with
buttered greaseproof paper.

In a heavy-based saucepan set over a
very low heat, melt 225g/8oz of the
chocolate with 2 tablespoons of water,
stirring frequently and occasionally
taking the pan off the heat to prevent
over-heating.

Once the melted chocolate is smooth,
stir in the caster sugar until dissolved.
Still working on and off the heat, stir in
the 175g/6½oz of butter, a little at a
time. Take off the heat. Sift in the flour
and work it in lightly. One by one,
work the egg yolks into the chocolate
mixture.

Whisk the egg whites with a pinch of
salt until firm. Fold these into the
chocolate mixture, using a large metal
spoon and working lightly with upward
movements. Then stir in the grated
orange zest.

Pour the mixture into the prepared
pan, knock it on a work surface a couple
of times to settle the contents and bake
for 40-45 minutes, without opening the
door for the first 20 minutes.

Check that the cake is cooking evenly
and turn the pan around if it is looking
lopsided. Turn up the oven setting to
190C/375F/gas5 and cook for a final 5
minutes. The cake should then be well
risen and firm. Insert the tip of a long
knife into the centre – it should come
out clean and dry.

Leave to cool in the tin for about 30
minutes, then carefully lift out and place
on a serving dish. Leave until cold.

Melt the remaining chocolate as
before, this time with 6 tablespoons of
water. Stir in the Cointreau, marmalade
and cream and sweeten with a little icing
sugar, if liked.

Take off the heat, stir in 1 tablespoon
of butter and pour over the cake. Use a
spatula to spread the coating evenly (it
will hide any defects and collapses – but
let the sauce dribble naturally down the
sides of the cake).

To serve, decorate the cake with some
of the soft fruit and mint sprigs. Heap
the rest of the fruit around the cake and
tuck in a few sprigs of mint. Put the
bowl of crème fraîche on the table with
the cake.

Left *Rich Chocolate Cake decorated with
mint and soft fruits.*

TRIBUTE TO AUNTIE NANCY

*the traditional English
Sunday Lunch*

MENU

FOR 6-8

*Roast Rib of Beef
Roast Potatoes
and Honeyed Roast Parsnips
Auntie Nancy's Yorkshire Puddings
Broccoli with Horseradish Butter
Sweet Glazed Carrots*

* * *

Lime Meringue Pie

TAKE a girl at the impressionable age of twelve . . . I quite fell in love with the English way of life when I first came to stay with friends of family friends in Cheshire. England and France were very different countries back then in the early Sixties. My English was so poor that I had to spend several minutes constructing polite sentences along the line of 'Does it snow here in winter?' Notebook in hand, however, I soon learnt (mostly by plodding through Agatha Christie with a dictionary, starting backwards with the ending to make quite sure I understood who had done it).

For me, it was the beginning of a long and happy relationship, not only with the family I stayed with, but also with England. This was the early Beatles era and it all seemed fabulously progressive to a well-brought-up French girl. One of the things I had been warned against was English food. There I had a pleasant surprise. Auntie Nancy, Mrs Campaigne, was an extremely good home cook, happy to teach her skills – which she had to do very patiently with me because of my limited vocabulary.

She frequently baked wonderful cakes that were quite unlike anything I had tasted in France – Dundee cake, Victoria sponge and, best of all, lemon meringue pie. For me, this was the crowning glory of the most elaborate and only formal meal of the week, Sunday Lunch. These are not quite Auntie Nancy's original recipes, but the following menu is a tribute to her.

TO DRINK: a Cabernet Sauvignon from California with the main course and a sweet still Vouvray white wine with the dessert. This latter choice is partly for old times' sake – when I was staying with Auntie Nancy and her family one summer, my parents sent a case of Vouvray by way of thanking them for putting up with their adolescent daughter. The wine duly arrived, but there was a huge duty to pay on it and my pocket money wouldn't quite stretch to so many pounds, shillings and pence . . . a truly embarrassing experience!

PLAN OF ACTION

The day before
Dessert: make and half-bake the pastry case

Earlier in the morning
Main course: bring meat to room temperature; trim and prepare vegetables; par-boil potatoes and parsnips
Dessert: make custard

About 1 ¾-2 hours before the meal
Main course: start cooking beef; make batter

About 1 hour before
Main course: start roasting potatoes and parsnips; cook carrots

About 20-30 minutes before
Main course: make Yorkshire Puddings; cook broccoli
Dessert: make meringue

Just before eating
Main course: carve beef and assemble vegetables
Dessert: bake meringue

ROAST RIB OF BEEF

1 rib roast of beef, weighing about 2.3k/5lb, at room temperature
2-3 tsp dry mustard
175ml/6fl oz red wine
1 level tbsp flour
150ml/ ¼pt beef stock
sea salt and freshly ground black pepper

Preheat the oven to 230C/450F/gas8.
Rub the beef with a little salt, plenty of pepper and dry mustard. Place on a rack over a roasting pan and roast for 20-25 minutes until well browned.

Now turn the heat down to 180C/350F/gas4. Continue roasting, basting occasionally and allowing about 15 minutes per ½ k/1lb for rare meat, 18 for medium, 22 for well done.

Take the pan out of the oven then collect and keep warm 5-6 tablespoons of the fat from the pan for the Yorkshire puddings. Pour 5 tablespoons of the red wine over the beef and return it to the oven for another 10-15 minutes. Remove from the oven and leave to settle in a warm place while baking the Yorkshire puddings.

To make the gravy: decant the fat from the top of the pan juices (it will probably leave only about 4 or 5 tablespoons of liquid). Stir in the flour with a wooden spoon and cook on the hob over a moderate heat for 2 minutes, stirring and scraping the bottom of the pan to get up the flavourful sediment.

Pour in the stock and the remaining wine and cook over a high heat for 2-3 minutes, stirring occasionally. Season and serve in a warmed sauce boat.

Right *Roast Rib of Beef and Yorkshire Pudding with Broccoli with Horseradish Butter and Sweet Glazed Carrots.*

AUNTIE NANCY'S YORKSHIRE PUDDINGS

MAKES 8 OR 9

115g/4oz flour
good pinch of sea salt
1 large egg
about 450ml/¾pt milk
oil, for greasing

About 40 minutes before the beef will be cooked, make the batter: sift the flour with the salt into a bowl. Make a well in the middle and break the egg into the well and add 1 tablespoon of the milk.

Using a wooden spoon, gradually work the flour into the central well, beating hard and adding the remaining milk a little at a time. Beat the batter until it is smooth and leave it to rest for at least 30 minutes.

Oil 8-9 Yorkshire pudding pans and keep them in a warm place.

When the beef is cooked, remove it from the oven and leave it to settle in a warm place. Turn the oven temperature up to 230C/450F/gas8.

Spoon 2 generous teaspoons of beef fat from the roasting pan into each greased pudding mould. Place them on a baking sheet and put them in the oven for a minute or two.

Remove them from the oven and pour about 2 tablespoons of batter into each tin. Bake near the top of the oven for 15-20 minutes, until the puddings are puffed up and golden. Serve at once.

Left *Traditional Sunday lunch is the perfect occasion for bringing out the best cutlery and china.*

ROAST POTATOES AND HONEYED ROAST PARSNIPS

900g/2lb even-sized waxy potatoes, peeled and halved
900g/2lb even-sized small parsnips, peeled
4-5 tbsp oil
1 tbsp runny honey
sea salt and freshly ground black pepper

Par-boil the prepared potatoes and parsnips in lightly salted boiling water for 6-10 minutes. Drain well and pat dry with paper towels or a clean tea-towel.

Score the parsnips and potatoes all over with a fork.

Pour 2-3 tablespoons of the oil into a roasting pan and heat through in the oven. When the pan is hot, take it out of the oven and season the oil with salt and pepper. Using kitchen tongs, turn the potatoes over in the oil until well coated.

Roast in the oven for about 1 hour, until crisp and golden on the outside and just soft inside, turning the potatoes over once or twice during roasting.

Once the potatoes are in the oven, prepare the parsnips: combine the remaining oil with the honey and season with salt and pepper. Brush the mixture over the parsnips and place in another small baking pan.

Add to the oven and roast for about 50 minutes until tender and golden, turning the parsnips over once or twice during roasting.

SWEET GLAZED CARROTS

675g/1½lb mature carrots, scraped and cut across on the slant into thick slices
1 tbsp oil
30g/1oz butter
½ tsp ground cumin
1 tsp caster sugar
sea salt and freshly ground black pepper

Bring a sauté pan of lightly salted water to a fast boil. Add the carrots and par-boil them for 5-6 minutes. Drain well.

Return the pan to a low heat, pour in the oil and swirl to coat. Add half the butter, followed by the carrots and stir to coat them well. Then sprinkle the carrots with the cumin and sugar. Cover and cook gently for 30 minutes, shaking the pan occasionally, until tender.

Turn up the heat, stir in the rest of the butter and cook for 1-2 minutes more, stirring. Serve hot.

BROCCOLI WITH HORSERADISH BUTTER

675g/1½lb broccoli, trimmed into even-sized florets with long thin stems
45g/1½oz softened butter
2 tsp creamed horseradish
sea salt and freshly ground black pepper

Bring plenty of lightly salted water to a rolling boil in a large saucepan. Add the broccoli and cook for 5-7 minutes until just cooked. Drain well.

In the same hot pan over a very low heat, combine the butter and horse-radish, stirring until the butter has melted. Return the broccoli to the pan and stir to coat it in the horseradish butter. Season with pepper and serve.

124

LIME MERINGUE PIE

4 unwaxed limes
3 scant tbsp cornflour
1 tbsp ground almonds
pinch of salt
115g/4oz caster sugar, plus more to taste
400ml/14fl oz boiling water
1 tbsp unsalted butter
4 egg yolks, lightly beaten
1 half-baked sweet shortcrust pastry shell
  (see page 85)

FOR THE MERINGUE:
3 egg whites
pinch of salt
170g/6oz caster sugar

TO SERVE:
300g/10 1/2oz raspberries
jug of cream or mixture of two parts
  fromage frais mixed with one part
  Greek-style yogurt, whisked with a little
  icing sugar

Preheat the oven to 200C/400F/gas6.
Finely grate the zest of 2 of the limes
and extract the juice from them all.

In the top pan of a double boiler,
using a wooden spoon, stir together the
cornflour, almonds, salt, sugar and the
boiling water. Occasionally putting the
pan in direct contact with the heat,
bring to the boil, stirring constantly.
Turn down the heat and simmer gently
for 10-15 minutes, stirring frequently.

Beat in the butter and the lime juice.
Keeping the pan over simmering water,
stir in the egg yolks and cook until
thick, stirring constantly (the custard
will curdle if you let it come to the
boil). Allow to cool a little and strain the
custard if necessary.

Stir the grated lime zest into the
custard. Check for sweetness and add a
little sugar, if wished. Pour the custard
into the prepared pastry case and leave
to settle.

Meanwhile, make the meringue:
whisk the egg whites with a pinch of salt
until they are stiff. Then whisk in the
sugar, 1 tablespoon at a time. Spoon the
meringue over the top of the tart,
fluffing it into wavy peaks with a fork.

Bake for 20 minutes, until golden
brown. If it is browning too fast, reduce
the heat a little. Leave to settle in the
oven for at least 10 minutes.

Serve warm or cold, surrounded by
raspberries and with a jug of cream or
fromage frais and yogurt mixture.

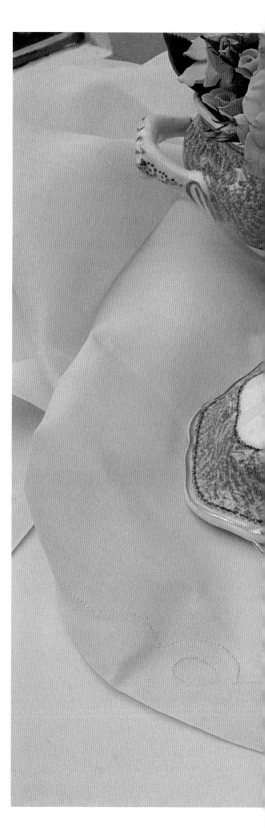

Right *A crisp pastry base, melting, rich
citrus filling, sweet soft topping – Lime
Meringue Pie is a multi-layered pleasure.*

INDEX